UNDERSTANDING
AND MENTORING
THE HURT TEENAGER

UNDERSTANDING AND MENTORING THE HURT TEENAGER

When Unconditional Love is Never Enough

Diana-Lea Baranovich

PARTRIDGE

Print information available on the last page.

To order additional copies of this book, contact
Toll Free 800 101 2657 (Singapore)
Toll Free 1 800 81 7340 (Malaysia)
orders.singapore@partridgepublishing.com

www.partridgepublishing.com/singapore

CONTENTS

CONTENTS

DEDICATION

This book is dedicated to all of you who work tirelessly to enhance the lives of hurt children and teenagers. Furthermore, I dedicate this book to the many teenagers with whom I have worked and who have taught me so much about the world of teenagers.

APPRECIATION

Much appreciation to my dear friend, Yun Yun, for her lovely art work shown on the front cover of this book.

FORWORD

It all started in the year 2000 when my family and I began working as volunteer foster care providers for Texas' Children's Protective Services. For those of you who haven't read my first book, **_Understanding and Caring for the Hurt Child: When Unconditional Love is Never Enough_**, I'll update you very briefly. During the years of 2000 – 2004, my family and I fostered several children of every shape, size and color between the ages of four to fifteen. We ventured into this altruistic endeavor with all the best intentions and compassion of Mother Theresa, Mahatma Gandhi and Princess Diana (*no, not me…the late Princess of Wales*) combined. I was also a doctoral student at the time, researching "at risk" children. In short, I was ready to be just what hurt children and teenagers need to make life-changing decisions; after all, I even had the theoretical knowledge. So…sprinkled on top of all this compassion was my academic arrogance.

Well, it was only a matter of hours (*honestly, not even days*) after our first foster child moved into our home that we quickly realized that not only is unconditional love never enough with hurt children and teenagers, but it is often resented by hurt children and teenagers. All of my academic arrogance flew out the window. I quickly realized that I, too, was a GI^2. By the way, GI^2 means Good Intentioned Idiot. Nonetheless, with endless fortitude and compassion, we continued to travel the journey of helping hurt children and teenagers for the next four years.

During these four years, my family and I came to understand the psyche of these children and why they (*who, for the most part, came from poverty stricken families of origin*) could not for the life of them embrace the opportunity of a family who was sincerely trying to help them move onward and upward in life. They would also call us every nasty name in the book (*even some out of the book*) and then ask for a new pair of shoes all within the same ten-minutes.

In short, hurt children and teenagers have entitlement issues that never end and never will without proper intervention. As mentioned in my first book, hurt children suffer from reactive attachment disorder (*now also known as disinhibited social engagement disorder*) usually co-morbid with oppositional defiance disorder, attention deficient hyperactivity disorder and in the worse cases, conduct disorder. OK…**OK**, enough of the psycho-bubble for now.

Putting the aforementioned aside, the children for whom we cared taught me more about the psychology of the hurt child (*also teenagers and adults for that matter*) and what they need more than any formal education could ever accomplish. It was surely the day-to-day observation and interaction with these children and teenagers that taught me what no textbook or research ever could. It is sort of like wanting to be a tennis player. Well…if you want to learn to play tennis, you will have to get a tennis ball and racquet and go on the court. You can't learn to play tennis by reading a book. If you want to learn about hurt children and teenagers, live with them or at least work very closely with them over an extended period of time. Believe me, they have a lot to teach you.

One of the first things I learned about these children and teenagers was how naïve they are about what it takes to sustain one's self in the adult world. Several of the children and teenagers, for whom we cared, lived in shelter homes before coming to live with us. I remember one innately intelligent fourteen-year-old girl who was under our care as part of the respite care program. Respite care is when a child from a shelter or foster care home lives with a sponsor family every other weekend and on holidays. I remember one Monday morning (*when she was spending the Thanksgiving holidays with us*) she asked on what days the food truck would be coming. I was flabbergasted. Did she really believe that a food truck was going to come and deliver free food that was donated by sponsors to my house as it does the shelter home? Well, yes, she honestly did. I explained to her that we have to buy our food with the money we earn from working. She sort of shrugged and said, "Oh" seeming very perplexed at the concept that food trucks do not stop and deliver food at everyone's house. This is just one of the many examples that I could share with you.

In short, there is nothing about shelter home or foster care living that prepares these children and teenagers to be self–reliant. So... how will they manage on their own when they turn 18 and have "outgrown" the system? The system has only served to condition them to expect handouts and donations. This, along with many other issues, places them at high risk for becoming welfare recipients or (*even more unfortunately*) criminals. However, as you will hear me say more than once, "All poodles are dogs, but not all dogs are poodles." All guilty criminals have entitlement issues (*it was OK for them to break the law and exploit other human beings*); however, not all people with entitlement issues become criminals.

What makes me say welfare recipients? Welfare is "handouts." Recipients of welfare don't earn the money they receive; it is just a handout. Although this has never been the intension of welfare programs, this is the reality of welfare programs. As I always say, "handouts breed entitlement." Then one day during those four years of foster care, I had a thought...out of the blue. I remembered a program in the states for disadvantaged preschoolers called the Head Start Program. This program began in the 1960's and is still going strong today. This program serves low socio-economic preschoolers between the ages of three to five. This is a state and federal funded program, which gives pre-school children enrichment experiences before they attend public school kindergarten. Such enrichment experiences include going to the zoo and regularly visiting the public library for reading enrichment experiences that they don't have in the home, among many other experiences. This program serves to help them start kindergarten with the same common experiences as their middle class and affluent counterparts.

So... I thought that it would be helpful to have a similar program for shelter home and foster care teenagers (*and other hurt and at risk teens as well*) to help prepare them for independent adult living. They need a head start program, which prepares them for post-secondary school life so that they will graduate and have more in common with "unhurt" teenagers. However, unlike the head start program, which is a school program, these teens need a one-to-one personal connection with someone. This would be a significant person who can guide them on an individual basis, as opposed to a group setting. Hence, I came up with the word "**mentor.**" Hurt teens need a mentor to facilitate their transition process into independent adult living.

Now, I must warn you that being a mentor for a hurt teen is very emotionally draining work; however, if you understand why these teenagers are the way they are, you will be in a much better place to help them. It first begins with understanding why hurt teenagers have self-sabotaging behaviors. Once you understand this, you can begin desensitizing yourself against their manipulative, abusive and entitled ways. Also, please allow me to remind you that although I have been referring to teenagers who have been raised in shelter home settings and foster care, hurt teenagers can be found in all walks of life. Some of them come from affluent homes where they live with their biological parents. It isn't the mere physical presence and financial support from a teen's parents that makes him immune to becoming hurt. It is the sincere, appropriate emotional connection, through all stages of child and teenage development, which serves to prevent teenagers from becoming hurt. Again, I must emphasize an "**appropriate**" emotional connection. Some parents have inappropriate emotional connections with their teenagers, and this is as equally damaging as physical abandonment and/or neglect. That being said, whether you are working with hurt teens whose parents have abandoned them or with hurt teens who live with their parents, it is not an easy row to hoe. I must be honest, if you are looking for a magic wand to wave to help these teenagers, close this book... **NOW**!!!

Likewise, if you are some one who has much experience with hurt teenagers and have found them to be mature, responsible, respectful and high functioning, close the book and contact me immediately. Just Google up my name on the nearest 21st century electronic gadget, and you will find me right away. We will co-author the book and begin doing workshops, immediately. I will give all due credit to you, and we will make immediate history and a fortune over night. Then we can donate the fortune to help support productive programs for hurt children, teenagers and even adults around the world. I am ready when you are. On the other hand, if the above has not been your experience, and you are looking to understand hurt teenagers and begin a very loooooooooooooooooong journey with them in their healing process (*one baby step at a time*), **Let's Go!!!!**

It is my hope, throughout this book, to break the 10 following myths many people have about hurt teenagers.

Myth One – *Teenagers are old enough to know better regardless of their upbringing. If a teenager is in trouble, it's up to him to begin making better choices.*

Yes, it is up to him to begin making better choices, but the hurt teenager is usually emotionally very much younger than his chronological age. Hence, he doesn't know where to begin making better choices because he doesn't know his options or what the different options are all about. If someone were to ask me if I would rather live with an indigenous tribe in Africa or an indigenous tribe in Papa New Guinea, this would be a difficult question for me to answer because I have no idea what living in either of these places would be like.

Myth Two – *Everyone has given up on him; he'll see that I am different, and he will trust me.*

Yes, he will see that you are different after a looooooooooooooooooooong, very looooooooooooooooooooong time. Meanwhile, he will test you like crazy and do every thing in the book (*and out of the book*) to have you give up on him. This is because he believes that you **WILL** give up on him and the sooner the better. So, be prepared for a lot of frustration during this looooooooooooooooooooong wait for him to trust you. The good news is that if you can weather the storm, he **WILL** begin to trust you sometime before you die of natural causes or the ozone layer completely disappears... patience, my friends.

Myth Three - *All teenagers go through rebellious stages, he will out grow this behavior.*

Hurt teenagers are different from their unhurt counterparts. Unhurt teenagers might go through a stage where they are testing the waters of authority figures; however, as soon as the authority figure lays down the law or reminds the teen of the law, the unhurt teenager will respect the rule and act accordingly, generally speaking. The hurt teenager will not so readily comply. Hurt teenagers are determined to be in control. Surely, the one thing that hurt teenagers are determined to have is **CONTROL.** If they don't get away with it using Plan A, they will quickly put Plan B into action.

Myth Four – *He's not lying to me because he trusts me.*

In most cases, lying has been a means of survival for the hurt teen. By lying, he has been able to avoid punishment, feel he is in control by "fooling" you and, in some way, get his needs met at that moment in time. This is a habit that the hurt teen has practiced for many years and has become very skilled. Breaking such a well-programed habit will take time and patience. However, confronting the lie in a non-threatening, supportive manner, at the time it is told, is the first step on the teen's journey of breaking this bad habit. Being angry, sarcastic or telling the teen that he will be damned to hell for lying or tell him he can't do this or that for a month because he lied will not help him quit lying. This will only make him re-evaluate his manipulative schemes and come up with better ones.

Myth Five - *I can trust him because we have a good rapport, and he would never betray me.*

Again, bad habits that have become a means of survival or have brought feelings of being in control to the hurt teen will not fade quickly or easily; such bad habits have become second nature. So... please hide your purse, your jewelry and other valuables when the hurt teen is around, and you are not there to watch them. If not, your money might go missing. May I remind you, this isn't anything personal, nor is it a sign that you are not helping the teen. Again, my friends, let me remind you about **PATIENCE.** Meanwhile, protect your belongings.

Myth Six - *God is the only one who can change him, I just need to insist that he go to the right church, mosque, synagogue, temple, shrine, fellowship house or some other holy place and put his troubles in God's hands.*

Hurt teens have no faith or trust in anyone, not even God. I have had hurt teens ask me, "Where was God when my Mom and Dad were beating me?"

"Where was God when we had to live in a car for three months because there was no money to pay rent." "Where was God when Mom dropped me off at the shelter home and never came back." Hurt teens are far from realizing how faith can be a support system. Lead by being a spiritual role model and not by attempting to bang any holy book over his head or force him to sit through any religious service that he isn't interested in attending. Whatever the message of the service is, it won't reach him anyway. This will just give him something else to resent you for; furthermore, it will weaken whatever rapport has been established between the two of you. Now, on the other hand, if the teen does feel connected to a certain spiritual path, celebrate it, encourage it and be thankful. Even if his spiritual path is different from yours, let this be fine. We are not here to convert, revert, change or rearrange anyone's spiritual beliefs or connections, short of the teen being involved in cults or organizations that are exploitative to the teen and society in general.

Myth Seven - *Having proper education is the answer to getting ahead in life. His academics are the most important aspect in his life, so he should forget about friends and activities for a while until he can pass school.*

Yes, there is a high correlation between higher levels of education and career advancement and income levels; however, let's put first things first. The teen must first believe in himself and see the need for education before he will (*even remotely*) begin to comprehend the importance of education. For most hurt teens, school has been just another place where there are a bunch of adult authority figures who don't understand them, call them belittling names, and tell them how lazy and naughty they are. Also, let's not forget the power of extra-curricular activities that the teen finds enjoyable and can serve as a platform for the teen to develop a sense of mastery and self–esteem. Having positive friendships and relationships with other peers can also go along way in the teen's journey of recovery. In short, don't get so carried away with academics that the other important aspects in life are overlooked.

Myth Eight - *He has never had nice clothes and things. I will treat him to a nice, name brand outfit. He'll really appreciate it.*

Yes, he will be happy for about a day, and then he will want something else. Hurt teens have entitlement issues. They don't really understand the concept of appreciation because they have never been appreciated. You will quickly become his personal Santa Clause, who is supposed to come bearing gifts with each visit. So... let the first step in teaching your teen appreciation be having him become appreciative of the relationship he has with you. He needs your connection and not material goods.

Myth Nine – *He knows his parents are very abusive toward him and are the cause of all of his problems in life. It's OK if I say this and remind him that it isn't his fault that his life hasn't worked out.*

Take this to the bank. There is an innate, unconditional love that every person on planet Earth has for his biological parents, especially his mother. Maybe it is different on Mars or Venus; my research hasn't extended that far, yet. For now, I am keeping my population narrow and only studying people on Earth. So... please don't ever say anything negative about the teen's birth parents or family members. He can talk bad about them, but no one else can. Even when he gets on a roll bashing his big bad mama, daddy, sister, brother, aunt, uncle or pet turtle, don't you dare join in that conversation. Just respond by saying something like, "Yes, it is very hurtful when the people who are suppose to love and care for us the most, hurt us the most."

Myth Ten – *Now that I have showed him the way, he will be able to avoid troubled people and stay out of trouble himself.*

Hopefully, after a looooooooooooooooooooooong period of time and many set backs he will; however, in the meantime, keep an eye on your teen. Hurt teens remain vulnerable for a very looooooooooooooong time. This is how powerful early programming can be.

May I also say, that although this book is written from the point-of-view of being a mentor for hurt teens, those of you who work with hurt teenagers in some capacity but do not wish to be mentors (*which is a very huge commitment*) will also find the information helpful. When we "understand the beast we are riding," we are better able to work less stressfully and in harmony with the "nature of the beast." Of course, I am using "beast" as a metaphor.

I would like to share my favorite quote.

"The events of childhood do not pass, but repeat themselves like seasons of the year."

Sister Eleanor Parjeon, Catholic nun who counsels inmates on death row in Angola, Louisiana (USA).

CHAPTER ONE

Who are the hurt teens and how do they become hurt?

Who are the hurt teens?

The term "hurt" refers to an emotionally hurt teenager, who is hurt due to abandonment, physically and/or emotionally, by the primary caregivers in his life. In most cases the teen was abandoned at a young age. However, the concept of abandonment is an infinitesimal continuum from a microscopic little bit to an endless amount. Simply put, the caregiver has not been appropriately emotionally available to the teen. This can also come from poor parenting skills; the teen's parents mean well, but they just don't know how to parent. Such a parent is what I call a GI^2 – remember, a Good Intentioned Idiot.

Because hurt teens are being raised under adverse conditions, they do not have the appropriate opportunities to explore and discover their interests, talents and proclivities, which allow them to develop a true sense of self. Hence, they develop a false sense of self. The false sense of self is usually filled with either a grandiose, unrealistic sense of self and one's capabilities or a highly underestimated sense of self and one's capabilities. Now, I will let you in on a secret; maybe you already know the secret. The teenagers who have a grandiose, unrealistic sense of self and capabilities are masking deep-rooted insecurities. Sometimes the teenager is aware of this; other times, he has completely "fooled" himself.

All teens are at risk of becoming hurt, not only due to emotionally unavailable caregivers but also by becoming involved in negative behaviors due to peer

1

pressure. Adolescence is a time of hormonal changes, identity formation, changes in societal roles, negative peer pressure and overall confusion. However, what intervenes in the teen's temptation to "act out" and participate in dangerous behaviors is a consistent, reliable support system. This support system does not have to be his biological parents. Based on my own clinical observations, the teen who has a caregiver or significant adult in his life who is consistently emotionally available to him will be less vulnerable to negative peer pressure.

Activity – Let's Explore

Let's see if we can recognize the signs of hurt teens and teens who are at risk of becoming hurt. Read the following case scenarios and think about who is a hurt teen and who is not. As for the teens who are not hurt, explain their sources of support. As for the teens who are hurt or at risk of becoming hurt, what is the cause and what resources of support do they need.

Discussions are on page 191 – no peeping.

NOTE: All of the following case scenarios are fictitious.

Teen A

Teen A is a 15-year-old boy. He lives in a lovely house in a nice gated community. Teen A has a younger sister, who is eight, and a dog named Spot. The family has a live-in housekeeper; she doesn't speak much English and just stays to herself most of the time. Teen A's father is a lawyer and his mother is an accountant for a private oil and gas firm. Teen A makes good grades in school and plays trumpet in the school band. His parents are saving money for his college fund and are letting him choose his course of study. Teen A's parents work long hours and are often away on overnight business trips. Last week, Teen A's Aunt Sally (*his mother's sister*) went to the school's band concert because both of Teen A's parents were out of town. Teen A was happy to have some one in the audience. Teen A has begun canceling his math tutoring sessions when his parents are out of town because he believes that he doesn't need them anymore, and the tutor is boring. Teen A would rather spend his time playing video games with his friends.

Teen B

Teen B is a 16-year-old girl. She lives in a low-cost housing project. She is the eldest of five siblings. Her four younger siblings are ages two, ten, twelve and thirteen. Teen B's father died of cancer five years ago. Teen B's youngest sibling (*who is actually her cousin*) is being raised by Teen B's mother because the toddler's mother has a drug problem and can't take care of him. Teen B's mother works as a cashier full-time at a nearby grocery store during the week, but she always stays home with the family on Saturdays and Sundays. Teen B's paternal grandmother also lives with the family and helps take care of the children. Teen B goes to school regularly; her grades are average. She enjoys school and hopes to be a teacher one day. Teen B has begun washing some of the neighbors' cars in order to save enough money to go on a camping trip with her church's youth group.

Teen C

Teen C is 17-year-old boy. He has recently been released from Juvie (Juvenile Detention Center). He has been in Juvie twice. The first time was when he was 13; he got caught breaking into a neighbor's house. The second time was for shoplifting DVD's from a department store. During his last stay in Juvie, Teen C was able to take a course in computer repair. He found this course to be very interesting and enjoyable. Teen C is now attending night classes to finish his high school diploma and working as an apprentice during the day at a computer repair shop. He still sees his friends on weekends; however, he now knows better than to get into any kind of trouble again. He has had enough of Juvie.

Teen D

Teen D is 14-year-old girl. She is a serious student who makes above average grades. She is involved in many extra-curricular activities such as sports, music, art and gymnastics. Her latest activity is playing on the chess team. She lives at home with her father, who is the manager of a construction company, and her mother, who is a part-time hairdresser at a salon. Teen D has a younger sister who is 12 and an older sister who is 16. She likes going on family trips to the beach, helping her mother cook and having sleepovers with friends.

Teen E

Teen E is a16-year-old girl. She is the youngest child of a very prominent family. Her father has been the city mayor for the past three years, and her mother is a very busy housewife. Mom is also the president of the city's garden club, very active in campaigning for Dad's political career, and has won many awards for her charity work during the past several years. Teen E's eldest brother has just started law school, and her older sister has a degree in marketing but is now a housewife. It is a family tradition for women to stay at home once they become mothers. Now that Teen E has had her 16th birthday gala, she can begin dating. It is also a long-standing family tradition to wait until the age of 16 to begin dating. Her mother's best friend's son will accompany Teen E to the Rotary Club's teenage ball next week. Teen E doesn't really like the boy; however, she knows that she will insult the family if she refuses to go. Teen E likes this guy in her class at school, but she knows that her parents would never approve of the two of them dating. The families do not get along; this has something to do with both of their fathers running against each other for city council years ago. So... Teen E just talks to him at school to keep the peace. *This sounds like Romeo and Juliet; I hope that it doesn't have a tragic ending.*

Teen F

Teen F is a 17-year-old boy. He is an only child from a single parent home. His mother left the family when he was two because she wanted to travel around Europe without distractions or responsibilities. Teen F has not heard from his mother since. Teen F's father works as both a waiter at a restaurant and a cashier at a large department store to make ends meet and pay bills. However, Teen F still spends quality time with his father. They go to movies, bowling and eat pizza together every weekend. When Dad mentions college, Teen F says that he wants to take at least two years off and join habitat for humanity. This is a volunteer organization that goes to underdeveloped communities and helps build and repair houses. Dad hasn't agreed to this yet, but Teen F hopes that he will.

Teen G

Teen G is a 15-year-old girl. She is from a mixed race family. Teen G's mom works as a kindergarten teacher and her dad works as a PE coach. She has a brother who is 17 and a twin sister. The family recently relocated to a new city because Dad transferred to another school district where the pay is better. All three siblings attend the same local high school. Teen G and her twin have many of the same classes together but tend to have different friends. Teen G notices that many of her classmates tend to skip classes and go to the track field for a smoke. Teen G wants to try smoking, but she was afraid to go home smelling like smoke.

Teen H

Teen H is a16-year-old boy. He has a sister who is 18 and a brother who is 14. His parents are currently separated and thinking about getting a divorce. Teen H thinks that this is for the best; all his parents ever do is shout and argue. His sister is attending nursing classes at his parents' insistence. The plan for Teen G is to join the military because his father is a Marine and wants at least one of the children to follow in his footsteps. Teen H thinks the military will be fun, especially learning how to fire guns. Teen H found out that his younger brother has begun smoking weed but has decided to mind his own business. Teen H doesn't want to give his parents anything else to blame each other for. Teen H also knows that his older sister doesn't really have night classes; she goes out with her friends to some club. Again, Teen H stays out of this; he just goes off into his room and surfs the web until it is time to eat.

Teen I

Teen I is a 13-year-old girl. She lives at home with her single mother. Mom has a new boyfriend, Fred, who seems a lot more responsible than the last one. This boyfriend holds a steady job as a construction worker. Mom works as a nurse's assistant at a nursing home. Mom has been working over-time lately to make extra money for the holidays. Fred is willing to drive Teen I and her younger siblings to school and sports practice. He even cooks super. Lately, Teen I has noticed that Fred likes to get right in her face when he speaks to her and rubs her back. This makes Teen I feel uncomfortable, but Fred surely is better and more responsible than the other guys mom has dated. It has been a long time since mom was this happy. So... Teen I has decided to remain quiet. The other day, Teen I went to use the home computer and noticed that Fred hadn't logged off. He was looking at websites for escort services.

Check discussions on page 191 and see if we agree.

At the end of every Chapter, I will include a few self-reflective questions. Of course, there are no right or wrong answers. I do this because it is very important for us as mentors, parents or significant adults (such as teachers, club leaders or coaches) to reflect upon not only our own teenage years but also what values we hold which influence (*in one way or another*) the way in which we work with hurt teens. As the saying goes, "We can't be all things to all people." When we are realistically in touch with our own values, talents, interests and proclivities, we are better able to know the "types" of teenagers (*as well as other people*) To whom we can be of the most help.

Self - reflective Questions:

1. What do you now know about hurt teens that you didn't know before?
2. Where did you lie on the hurt teen scale when you were a teenager?
3. To what extent were your parents/caregivers there for you, emotionally, during your teenage years?
4. If you have children and/or teenagers, are you there emotionally for them? Are there times when you believe that you need to be more emotionally present for them?
5. Think of the teenagers that you presently know in your life; which ones are hurt and in what way? What are the parents/caregivers doing or not doing which is causing the teen to be hurt?
6. Of the above aforementioned teens, which teen do you believe you would be the most suited to help? Explain.

CHAPTER TWO

The Teenage Years: Developing a Sense of Self

A Sense of Self is merely one's understanding of himself in all aspects of life. What one likes and dislikes, what one is does well and does not do well, the friends one keeps, the job one performs, and what one feels he has to contribute to the world.

Self - understanding, is another term for sense of self, Harter explained that self-understanding is an individual's cognitive representation of himself, the substance and content of his self – conception.

Harter (2006). *The Self: Social, Emotional and Personality Development – A Handbook of Child Psychology.* John Wiley and Sons, Inc. USA.

Teenagers carry with them (*24-7-365- including public holidays*) a sense of who they are and what makes them different from everyone else. Whether this sense of self is real, imagined, exaggerated or totally fabricated, a teen's sense of self becomes the pre-dominate motivating factor for all aspects of his life. Following are actual conversations that I had with four different teenagers in order to gage each one's sense of self.

Activity - Let's Explore

Which of the teen's below have a realistic, true sense of self and which do not? Explain.

Teen 1

I asked a high functioning 16-year-old boy from a very supportive family to describe himself.

Boy: I am an extroverted, people-oriented person. I am tall and thin, and I am the third of four children, two girls and two boys. I live in an upper-middle class suburb. My favorite subjects in school are math and physics. I am very dedicated to my studies. I plan to go to a national university and major in mechanical engineering. I am also on my school's swim team and basketball team. When I am not studying or at sports practice, I am busy making things. I have a talent for building things out of wood, such as tables and cabinets. My grandfather wants me to market my original wood furniture some day. Would you like to see some of the tables I just finished?

Me: I'd love to. *He pulled out his phone and showed me the picture of a dinning room table and six chairs that he recently finished making and explain the type of wood and the sanding technique he used.* It's beautiful.

Teen 2

I asked a well-behaved, 16-year-old boy from a shelter home to describe himself.

Boy: My name is XXXX, and I am 16. *He at that point didn't have anything else to say. Hence, I began to ask specific questions.*

Me: What are your favorite hobbies?

Boy: Gaming. *He then explained that he meant playing video games.*

Me: What are your favorite subjects in school?

Boy: Not sure.....maybe geography.

Me: What about geography do you like?

Boy: The teacher is nice.

Me: Are you involved in any extra-curricular activities at school?

Boy: I was on the soccer team for a while, but then I had to quit because I failed three subjects and had to go to tuition classes.

Me: Did you enjoy playing soccer?

Boy: Yes.

Me: Would you like to be on the team again?

Boy: Yes (*his face lit up like a Christmas tree*) but first, I have to be passing all subjects.

Me: Hopefully that will happen soon, so you can get back on that field. *He twisted his lips and raised his eyebrows, as if he didn't have much faith in this happening.*

Me: Any ideas about what you'd like to do after secondary school?

Boy: No, not sure, but I've been thinking about it.

Me: When you think about it what comes to your mind?

Boy: Living with my dad again.

Me: OK... any thoughts about a job or higher education.

Boy: Well, my dad works at a gas station. He can probably get a job for me there. I don't think I want to go to college or anything. *We then began to talk about working at a gas station would be like – all in a positive way.*

Teen 3

I asked a well-behaved 16-year-old shelter home girl to describe herself.

Girl: I am an Indian girl from a large family. I am very friendly, and I have lots of friends.

Me: What do you like to do with your friends?

Girl: We like to watch singing and dancing shows like American Idol and Voice. We like to teach each other dances and sing Karaoke.

Me: Any thoughts about what you would like to do when you graduate from secondary school?

Girl: I'd like to work in a bridal shop.

Me: What about working in a bridal shop appeals to you?

Girl: I like the pretty dresses and doing the brides hair and make-up. *We continued discussing bridal shop work.*

Teen 4

I asked a high-functioning, 15-year-old girl from a home with very supportive parents to describe herself.

Girl: I am a 17-year-old Chinese girl whose horoscope is Gemini, and I am getting ready to finish Form 5 (*last year of high school*).

Me: Can you share some things that you like about school.

Girl: I like school overall. My favorite classes are English and Math. I don't like history. Most of the teachers are pretty good.

Me: Do you participate in any extra-curricular activities?

Girl: I am on the debate team.

Me: Tell me about your debate team?

Girl: I love it. I like to research the topics and meet friends from other schools.

Me: Any thoughts about what you would like to do after secondary school?

Girl: I hope to study medicine overseas.

Me: When did you realize that you wanted to study medicine?

Girl: My parents have been sacrificing and saving money all their lives for me to study medicine.

Me: What about becoming a doctor attracts you to the profession.

Girl: It is a respectable job, and I would make a good living. *We talked a bit more about the medical profession.*

Check discussions on Page 195 and see if we agree.

Adolescence marks the beginning of Eric Erickson's 5th stage of psychosocial development.

Stage Five: Identity vs. Role Confusion

"Adolescents seek to develop a coherent sense of self, including the role he or she is to play in society. Higher education and career choices become very difficult without a strong sense of personal identity."

Erickson, E. (1968). *Identity: Youth and Crisis,* W. W. Norton & Company, USA.

I have come to understand Erikson's 5th stage as being the beginning stage of forming one's authentic identity. As adolescents journey through their teenage years, they begin to "explore and discover" and ultimately ascertain and organize their abilities, proclivities, needs, interests, gender identity, sexual orientation and desires into their innate personalities in order to express themselves appropriately and productively in society. In short, the adolescent develops a sense of self. We want this sense of self to be an authentic and realistic, true sense of self.

Although identities form throughout a person's lifetime, Erikson's theory suggests that the adolescent years mark the beginning of a life long journey of identity formation, providing Stages 1 - 4 have been successfully completed.

Generally speaking, where hurt teenagers are concerned, Stages 1 – 4 have not been successfully completed; hence, appropriate backtracking is essential. However, at the same time we are backtracking, we also need to help hurt teenagers prepare for independent adult living. In short, folks, it is double duty. I will explain more about helping hurt teens backtrack through Stages 1 – 4 in Chapter 7.

As mentioned earlier, developing a sense of self requires self-understanding. A person's authentic sense of self, which is his self-understanding, begins during his pre-teen years. The adolescent's sense of self is based upon his childhood upbringing, his environment and the extent to which he has opportunities to explore and discover activities and come to know what interests him in his life. In turn, all of the aforementioned serve to mold his level of self-esteem and his self-concept, which he will carry forth into his adult years.

Throughout his adolescent years, a teenager's sense of self is based upon the various roles he plays and the groups to which he belongs. During the early teenage years, the teenager begins to develop a sense of what makes him "tick" and how his interests, talents and proclivities serve him. By his late teens, his sense of self then translates into how he pictures himself in the adult world. The bottom line is that adolescents will develop a sense of self; this sense of self will be either a true sense of self or a false sense of self. Carl Rogers argued that if there is a strong discrepancy between the person's real self (*true self*) and what the person perceives himself to be (*false self*), the person will become maladjusted. The person will either develop an overly grandiose sense of self, which he will not be able to live up to, or he will undermine his capabilities and develop a sense of failure and self-criticism; either can trigger depression.

Rogers (1950). *The Significance of the Self- Regarding Attitude and Perceptions.* McGraw Hill: New York.

When considering emotionally healthy teenagers, it is normal for younger teens (*12 to 14 years*) to have more idealistic views of the self, which might not be grounded in reality. For example, the short, overweight young teenager might have dreams of being a New York runway model. The emotionally healthy teen (*15 to 19 years*) has a more realistic, true sense of self. As the young teen grows into late adolescence, it will be important for her to see herself realistically and come to realize that she doesn't have the body type to be a New York runway model. If she doesn't come to realize that her 5 feet 2 inch body doesn't accommodate her dream of becoming a model and accept this, she will be doomed to rejection.

It is important to remember that the hurt teen will have a tendency to hold on to his idealistic, false sense of self. He will not be able to relate to himself in a realistic manner. This is about self-protection, which is also very important during the adolescent years. This stems from social comparison and social consciousness. In an attempt to protect themselves, adolescents tend to deny their negative characteristics, limitations and what they feel is inadequate about their social standing. Simply put, hurt teenagers become very aware of what they lack in life as compared to their healthier peers. This is known as social comparison. Their private self becomes very hidden from the view of others. This is often times accomplished through their personal fables. I have found that many adolescents who are insecure, have low self- esteem and are not proud of who they are or from where they come tend to make up personal fables.

So what is a personal fable?

The Origins of the Term "Personal Fable"

David Elkind (1931 – present) is an American child psychologist. Elkind was the first to coin the term "personal fable" in his 1967 book *Egocentrism in Adolescence.* Elkind's theory of adolescent development is built upon Piaget's theory of adolescent development, which describes how teenagers do not accurately differentiate themselves from others during the early teenage years. The young teenager's (*12-14 years*) thoughts and beliefs about self-perception are not rooted in reality. The young teenager believes that he is very unique and that other's see and are obsessed with him as he is obsessed with himself. Building upon Piaget's theory that young teenagers' perceptions of themselves are not rooted in reality, Elkind used the term "personal fable" to describe the untrue stories adolescents tell themselves about their place in the world.

Elkind, D. (1967). *Egocentrism in Adolescence.* **Published by Wiley behalf of the Society for Research in Child Development.**

I would like to take Elkind's concept of the adolescent personal fable a step further to include the stories about themselves that teenagers (*young or old*) tell other people. This aspect of the personal fable is a person's own made up story about his life or some aspect of his life. This always comes from a place of insecurity within the person. This can be common during the early adolescent years; however, it is likely to carry over well into the late adolescent years and even into the adult years if the adolescent does not begin to develop a healthy sense of high self- esteem and a true, realistic sense of self.

For example, countless times when I was working as a school psychologist, I would have a teenager come in for his weekly appointment. I would smile and say, "Hi Johnny (*not his real name*), how was your weekend?" The child would answer, "Oh, my dad picked me up and we went to the movie, ate pizza, he bought me a new pair of Nike's (*meanwhile the child is still wearing the same old shoes*) and we went to the theme park. He is going to come get me again this weekend.

The truth of the matter is Johnny's father has been in jail for the past 10 years. The adolescent creates personal fables as a way of dreaming and feeling better about himself. He feels better about himself because he believes that the listener believes him and believes that he is better off in life than he actually is. It is all a defense/coping mechanism. This is a major part of developing a false self. This is an example of a "big" personal fable. Personal fables come in all different shapes and sizes. Some are small; for example, when someone says that he has a 3.8 cumulative grade point average when, in fact, he has a 3.3. This is a small personal fable and there are many in between sizes. I will share my personal fable that stayed with me from the ages of 12 to 17. I apologize to any of my university students who have heard this story before (*probably more than once*) during one of my classes.

My adolescent personal fable was…"My dad's a geologist." In reality my late father worked as a draftsman for Shell Oil Company for 35 years. I grew up the youngest of three children in a comfortable middle class home during the 60's and 70's. My father made a comfortable living. However, I remember my father saying from time to time that he wished he were a geologist. This came from a place of enjoying the subject matter and not a desire to make more money. However, I do remember as a young girl going over to the houses of my father's geologist colleagues from time to time and noticing that their houses were always bigger and in neighborhoods that were a step or two up from my neighborhood. Thus, this set in me the early programing that geologists are richer, more educated and of higher standing than draftsmen.

When I was twelve, I remember whenever my friends or anyone asked me the typical conversational question, "What does your dad do?" I would answer, "He's a geologist." This personal fable stayed with me for the next five years. I remember the day in May of 1979 after I graduated from high school (*I am 55; put your calculators away, please*) when I laid my personal fable to rest, naturally. During those summer months, I dated a guy before I began university. He asked me on our first date "What does your dad do?" I answered, "He is a draftsmen." I thought to myself... Wow, I told the truth. Hence forth, I would always answer, "My dad is a draftsman." I had reached a stage in my life where I no longer needed the personal fable to feel better about myself. It was no longer important for me to believe that others thought my family was of higher economic and social standing than we were. I was secure within myself. Well, as the story continues....I married a geologist. Really, I did; it's not a personal fable...early programming....maybe?

Now, let's be honest. Adults have personal fables as well. Have you ever heard an adult say his salary is 5000 dollars a month when in reality his salary is 3,500 dollars a month. No confessions needed, my dears...I rest my case.

The bottom line is that people have personal fables to either avoid facing something they feel is unpleasant or substandard in their lives and/or make themselves appear more important, richer or better in some way than they actually are because they believe that their "true life situation" is inadequate. Hurt teens will have personal fables. When working with hurt teens, it is important to recognize their personal fables and help the teen see himself in a more honest way. Also, the main ingredient of working with hurt teens is helping them to develop a healthy, true sense of self. This will be an outgrowth of helping the teen build his self-esteem. As the teen's self-esteem is enhanced, his personal fables will begin to fade; it's automatic.

I must also add that, at times, parents make up personal fables about their children. For example, a parent tells his teenage son to tell his relatives that he made the honor roll at the family dinner this Saturday. In reality the teen did not make the honor role; however, this personal fable will make the parent feel "better" about himself as a parent. Sometimes, this has to do with "keeping up with the Jones' family;" meaning, if the Jones' teenager makes the honor roll, our teenager can't appear inferior to the Jones' teenager.

Behavioral Indicators of Self-esteem

There is a high correlation between personal fables and self-esteem. There is also a high correlation between high self-esteem and an emerging true sense of self. Therefore, in order to have any hope of a teenager growing into a person with a true sense of self, it is important to understand his level of self-esteem.

Positive Indicators of High Self-esteem

Based on my own clinical observation, I have found the following traits to be associated with teenagers who have high self-esteem.

A teenager with high self-esteem will tend to …

- express opinions with confidence;
- have voice tone and language appropriate for the situation;
- sit with his peers during social activities;
- happily explore new activities to see if they are of interest to him;
- be able to develop appropriate rapport with adults;
- work cooperatively in a group;
- be able to be a good follower, as well as a good leader;
- face others when speaking or being spoken to;
- maintain eye contact during conversations;
- not be afraid to ask for help;
- not be afraid to tell the truth even when it means he might get into trouble;
- not be afraid to admit that he doesn't understand something;
- initiate appropriate, friendly contact with others;
- maintain comfortable space between self and others;
- have little hesitation in his speech and speak fluently;
- learn from his mistakes.

Negative Indicators of Low Self – esteem

Based on my own clinical observation, I have found the following traits to be associated with teenagers who have low self-esteem.

A teenager with low self-esteem will tend to...

- put down others by teasing, name-calling or gossiping;
- use gestures that are dramatic or out of context;
- engage in inappropriate touching or avoid physical contact;
- give excuses for his failures;
- brag excessively about achievements, skills and appearance (*personal fable*);
- verbally put himself down (*self-depreciation*);
- speak too loudly, abruptly or in a dogmatic tone;
- float around from peer group to peer group trying to find a place to fit in;
- be at risk of becoming a loner and spending all day shut up in his room;
- be at risk of becoming addicted to social media;
- be vulnerable to unhealthy peer groups;
- change clothes and hairstyles, often, as an attempt to find himself.

Needless to say, teenagers with high self-esteem tend to have a healthy, true sense of self.

A teenager with a healthy, true sense of self will tend to...

- tell the truth about his accomplishments in life;
- realistically understand his strengths and limitations;
- feel secure in making his own decisions about his style of clothing and what groups to join;
- have a sense of morals and values;
- have a positive outlook on life
- have parents (*usually*) who consistently practice bonded parenting; I will explain more about parenting styles in Chapter 8.

In summary, when someone feels secure and self-confident, he is living from a true self. Teenagers who evolve into an ego state of identity achievement are living out of a true self. This will be further explained in Chapter 6.

The False Self

After 30 years of clinical experience, I have come to know that **ALL** teenagers create a sense of self. Hurt teenagers tend to develop a false sense of self and seek love and belonging in the wrong places and with the wrong people. On the other hand, healthy teenagers develop a true sense of self and find acceptance and belonging in the right places and with the right people.

A teenager with a false sense of self will have a tendency to ...

- change attire, hairstyles, morals and opinions to suit the group he is a part of or wants to become a part of;
- exaggerate or lie about aspects of his life, such as saying he lives in a three-story house with a private pool. In reality, he lives in a low-cost flat (*personal fable*). Another example would be - saying he won second place at the science fair. When in reality, he didn't even enter the fair (*personal fable*).

Another example of living through a false self would be the teenager whose parents make all the decisions for him; such as, telling him where he will attend college, what he will study, who his friends should be and so on. In short, the teenager is not being allowed to make decisions based upon his own interests or how he has come to know himself. Another example would be a girl, as a result of being sexually abused or harassed, decides to cut her hair very short to make herself less attractive to men.

In short, when someone feels insecure, he lives through a false self in an attempt to hide his insecurities. I think of the false self as a persecutor in the disguise of a protector. For example, an attractive girl who makes herself look ugly is persecuting herself by denying herself the pleasure of celebrating her authentic attractive appearance; however, her ugly false self protects her from having men pay attention to her.

Self - reflective Questions:

1. Take a walk down memory lane and remember as much as you can about your teenage years. Did you have any personal fables? If so, what purpose did these serve for you? How long did you tell the personal fable?

2. As an adult do you have any personal fables? Shhhhhh….. I promise not to tell. If so, what do you see as the need for having these fables? What might people think if you begin to tell the truth instead of your fable?

3. Have you known teenagers who have personal fables? How do you react when you hear a teen's personal fable?

4. By the end of your teenage years, were you a teen with a true, healthy sense of self?

5. Where do you believe you are now in terms of a true self vs. a false self?

From Diana's Pearls of Wisdom – The false self is always a persecutor in the disguise of a protector. As long as we live through a false self, we deprive ourselves and the world of our innate gifts and uniqueness.

CHAPTER THREE

Attachment Theory (In a nut shell)

Teenagers don't just wake up one morning at the age of sixteen or so with either a true or false sense of self. Their sense of self has been continuously evolving (*24-7-365-including public holidays*) since birth. So, what are the factors that contribute to a teenager becoming a person who is capable of developing ongoing healthy, reciprocal relationships with others? Unlike the teenager who develops a false sense of self, and therefore has difficulties developing ongoing healthy, reciprocal relationships, the teenager with a true sense of self has had the advantage of being genuinely validated for his unique, individual self.

It is all about what happened between the teenager and his primary caregiver during his first five years of life; most importantly is what happened during his first year of life. This whole concept of true vs. false self is rooted in my favorite theory, which all of my ardent fans and faithful followers know by now is John Bowlby's attachment theory. Teenagers, who develop a true sense of self, are raised by parents or caregivers with whom they have a healthy, secure base attachment. Such parents encourage their children to be secure and understand who they authentically are, including understanding their strengths and their limitations. It is a bonus if such children and teenagers also have other significant adults in their lives who also sincerely validate them. This surely contributes to their cultivation of a true sense of self.

John Bowlby stated, "There is a strong causal relationship between an individual's experience with his parents and his later capacity to make affectional bonds."

Bowlby, J., Separation, *Anxiety and Anger*, 1973, The Tavistock Institute of Human Relations, USA.

The most important year of life that determines our level of attachment is the first year of life. During the infant's first year of life, he has the right to be the total boss of the household. No one else's needs, wants or issues are of any concern to him. He gets what he wants, when he wants it 100% of the time (*with no exceptions*) all day everyday, including public holidays. A baby who experiences this during his first year of life develops a secure base attachment to his primary caregiver. On the other hand, infants who experience inconsistent care giving do not develop a secure base attachment.

What do I mean by inconsistent care giving, you ask? I mean the infants, and also young toddlers, who don't always get their diaper changed or feed or held or rocked on demand. Instead the infant or young toddler is left in his crib to "cry it out." After all, you don't want to spoil him. Truth is, you can't spoil an infant or young toddler. An infant or young toddler is not capable of understanding waiting because other people have needs. Nor is he capable of understanding such concepts as sharing, compromise, consideration for the needs of others, delayed gratification or empathy. To expect (*in the least*) such understanding and compassion from a child less than the age of three to four is completely developmentally inappropriate. Why don't we just send him to Harvard and hope he learns algorithms… get the picture?

All babies and young toddlers of the world are entitled to their primary narcissism during the first three years of life. Interestingly enough, the babies and young toddlers who have their primary narcissistic needs met during the first two to three years of life, are the ones who are learning to trust. They also develop a conscience and the ability to empathize with others. He is learning that his needs will be met and the world (*within his home environment*) is a safe place. In turn, he will transfer this positive attitude and trust in people to the community outside of his home environment. Now, hang on, please. I know you are thinking…but isn't this dangerous because some people are bad and some places aren't safe. This is true. So… the next step in appropriate parenting is to teach preschoolers about personal safety and discrimination when talking to strangers. On the other hand, babies and young toddlers who don't consistently have their needs met, do not learn to trust, nor do they develop a conscience or the ability to empathize with others. They remain emotionally stuck in that egocentric stage of toddlerhood where everything is about me, Me, ME, **ME**... I want, I Want, **I WANT - NOW!!**

In short, chronologically they move on and become three, four, five, twenty-six, sixty-six... but.....they still have not grown emotionally. Society will expect them to act their age; when in reality, they can't. So... here comes the negative labels from the teachers, coaches and other adults in their lives, such as you are naughty, bad, lazy, mean to your friends, never put out any effort and so on.

VERY IMPORTANT – CAREGIVER MONOGAMY

I must also add that babies and toddlers, (*even pre-school children*) much prefer caregiver monogamy. Meaning, they want one primary caregiver to cling to and bond with. They do not want mama on weekends, grandma during the week and/or uncle Joe and Aunt Betty for a few days while Mom and Dad go on holiday to an exotic island.

Let's think about it. You are happily married to your spouse; At least, for the moment, let's imagine that you are happily married to your spouse. One day you come home and your spouse tells you that he or she will be very busy with a work project over the next few months and won't be physically or emotionally available for you; therefore, he or she has decided to lend you his or her best friend to act as your spouse (*in all respects*) for the next few weeks. How do you feel? Well... to a young child, the primary caregiver is his lover and no one else can take that person's place...get it?

This all goes hand in hand with Eric Erickson's first stage of psychosocial development, trust vs. mistrust, which actually means secure attachment vs. insecure attachment.

Stage One: Trust vs. Mistrust

"If an infant's needs are consistently met, he learns to trust the people and his environment. If the infant's needs are not met, he learns to mistrust."

Erickson, E. (1975). *Childhood and Society*. Penguin Books, USA.

When an infant, during his first year of life, has **ONE** consistent primary caregiver to cling to, who appropriately responds to his needs (*24-7-365-including public holidays*), the baby learns to trust that people will meet his needs. The baby also begins to develop a conscience and empathy toward others. On the other hand, if the baby, during his first year of life, experiences inconsistent care or is shuffled around among several caregivers, he does not learn to trust. A sense of mistrust begins to develop; this impedes upon his ability to develop a conscience and the ability to empathize with others.

Go to any prison or juvenile detention center, and you will see people who did not develop a conscience or the ability to empathize with others. Now hold on a minute, all poodles are dogs but not all dogs are poodles. All guilty prisoners lack conscience; however, not all people who lack conscience become prisoners. I say "guilty" prisoners because, as we know, sometimes the innocent are wrongfully accused. On the other hand, yes, guilty prisoners lack conscience; people with a conscience do not rob, rape, kill, blow up buildings, etc.

What if a baby does not develop a secure base attachment during his first year of life?

Psychiatrist, Foster Cline, explains that if a secure base attachment does not develop during the first year of life, there are two windows of opportunity to build a secure base attachment. However, it takes total dedication and understanding on behalf of the caregiver. The first window of opportunity is between 12 months to 36 months. Generally speaking, up until the age of three, a secure base attachment can be developed with a lot of patience, perseverance, persistence and prayer (*four P's and a teaspoon*). I will be explaining more about the teaspoon in the next chapter. The second window of opportunity is between the ages of three to six years; however, it is far more difficult. Unfortunately, some children pass the age of six have been so abused and neglected that it is already too late. The clay becomes very hard after the age of six.

Cline, F. (1979). *Understanding and treating the severely disturbed child.* Evergreen Consultants in Human Behavior. CO. USA

Do you remember the seven-year-old boy who was adopted from an orphanage in Russia by an American family in 2010; it was all over international news. You can see still find it on YouTube. The boy was being cruel to animals and threatening to kill people and burn down houses. The adoptive parents put the child on a plane, alone, with a note of explanation and sent him back to Russia. This caused much international controversy. Unfortunately, with this child, the clay was already too hard. However, with many children, it won't be too late. Let's not give up; it's 4P's and a teaspoon, folks. Again, more on teaspoons in the next chapter.

I must also mention that it is easier if the bonding process is taking place between the birth parents and the child. It will be far more difficult with foster and adopted children and their foster and adoptive parents.

So, what do we do with unattached, hurt teenagers? Should we bother? Of course we should. Here is the difference. First of all, a mentor is not trying to adopt the teenager and have him "blend" into the family and build a bond with his caregiver and other family members. The mentor's role is to help enhance the teen's self-esteem, self-confidence and discover his talents, interests and proclivities. This is a very different job description. You will still have to build trust and rapport because they do have "attachment issues" to one degree or another, but again, this is a very different relationship than adoption.

From my first book, ***Understanding and Caring for the Hurt Child,*** here are the signs of attached and unattached teenagers.

An unattached teenager will tend to…

- have poor eye contact;
- lie;
- be rebellious toward authority;
- lack empathy and remorse;
- be at risk for substance abuse;
- skip school;

- be at risk for early sexual behavior because he is looking for validation and a sense of love and belonging;
- in the overwhelming majority of cases, develop a false sense of self, including many personal fables;
- in some cases, be overly compliant.

In reference to the overly compliant teenager, please do not be fooled. He doesn't have any fewer problems than the "acting out" teenager; he is harboring a lot of implosive anger. One day the volcano will erupt. When this happens, hope that you are not in his line of fire. These are the teens we see on the news who go into schools and open random fire on people then kill themselves. Sometimes they commit suicide without committing homicide; other times, they commit homicide without committing suicide. Again, hope that you are somewhere far away.

So… beware of the overly compliant, quiet teenager. Don't let him fall between the cracks.

A caregiver of a teenager who does not attach will tend to.

- not get involved with the teen's activities and interests, such as school clubs and extra curricular activities;
- not attend school events or seek activities in the best interest of the teen;
- not enhance autonomy building;
- rescue and protect the teen, such as doing the teen's homework so he doesn't get a failing grade or lies for the teen and says that he stayed home from school because he was sick when the teen was truant;
- make all decisions for the teen;
- have poor guidelines or puts too many restrictions on the teen;
- use discipline that is too unfair or inconsistent;
- assign chores or set limits that are not appropriate, fair or consistent;
- engage in battles and power struggles; there is no mutual respect or communication;

- not differentiate what the teen is capable of doing independently vs. what the teen needs help with;
- neglect the teen emotionally and/or physically because the caregiver is over involved with his own live and issues.

An attached teenager will tend to...

- smile and look at others in the eye;
- search for autonomy and is pleased to explore and learn new things;
- allow others to share leadership and control;
- be able to make age appropriate decisions;
- seek out relationships with other positively productive people;
- be positive about his future.

A Caregiver of an attached teenager will tend to ...

- consistently practice bonded parenting;
- have high self-esteem;
- enjoy parenting;
- know where the teen is, with whom and what he is doing without spying on the teen or being a helicopter parent (*helicopter parents hover over the teen at all times*).
- celebrate the unique individuality of the teen;
- participate in the teen's schooling and extra-curricular activities;
- encourage the teen to choose his own hobbies;
- encourage the teen to choose his own higher education, job training and/or career path;
- not live vicariously through the teen;
- listen to the teen with an open mind;
- insist that the teen own his own behavior and not rescue the teen.

Baranovich, *Understanding and Caring for the Hurt Child* (2013); Pearson Publishers, Malaysia.

Activity – Let's Explore

Below are scenarios of three different teenagers' first day of high school.

All three teenagers are from upper-middle class, professional families. They live in the same neighborhood. They are all 14 years of age and attend the same high school. They all make average to above average grades in school. They are all excited about starting their first year of high school. However, they each have different levels of attachment to their parents. Below are cases scenarios of the evening of their first day of high school.

Which teenagers are securely attached to their parents and which are not? Explain.

NOTE: All of the following case scenarios are fictitious.

Teen X – It is your first day of high school. You are full of enthusiasm. You made very good grades in primary and middle school, and you are excited about starting high school. You plan to take advanced level science, math and English, join clubs and play sports.

Teen Y – It is your first day of high school. You are full of enthusiasm. You made very good grades in primary and middle school, and you are excited about starting high school. You plan to run in the school government elections, join the band and play sports.

Teen Z - It is your first day of high school. You are full of enthusiasm. You made very good grades in primary and middle school, and you are excited about starting high school. You plan to take Japanese as your foreign language, advanced math, join the tennis team and drama club.

Teen X – It is the evening of your first day of high school. The family is sitting down at dinner and your father asks how your first day of school went. You explain that you had a great day and that your teachers are cool, your best friend from middle school is in your algebra class, you have decided to join the drama club and have chosen art as your first year elective. This leads to a family discussion about what types of art projects you will be doing.

Teen Y - It is the evening of your first day of high school. You are sitting in your living room playing your new X Box game when your father walks in. You are not sure where mom is. Sometimes she comes home before 9:00 PM and sometimes not. She mentioned something about meeting a friend to sell Mary Kay cosmetics. Whatever… last month she was thinking about selling Tupperware and a few months before that she was taking a leisure-learning course in Tarot card reading. Your father walks in and says, "Hey" as he walks into the kitchen to get a drink. He comes in and tells you to finish the game because he wants to watch television. You turn off your X Box and tell your father that you have decided to join the newspaper club at school and have signed up for art as your first year elective. Your father tells you (*as he begins to flip through the channels with his remote*) that the newspaper club is too time consuming. Your math grades fell 10 marks during the last marking period. Your father has arranged for you to have math tuition after school everyday for two hours. This sounds fine to you. You'll pull up your math grade this first term and then ask him about joining the newspaper club next term.

Teen Z - It is the evening of your first day of high school. You are sitting at the dinning room table organizing your notebooks. Your father comes home from work and announces that Mom called today and announced that she has been promoted to senior manager at the accounting firm where she has been employed for the past ten years. Everyone is excited. Your father asks you if you would like to join him and your mom for dinner at Mom's favorite seafood restaurant. You think this is a great idea. You were planning on going by your friends house to check out his new racing bike, but this can wait for another day. You immediately call your friend with apologies. While at the restaurant, you congratulate your mom and ask her what the new job assignment will be like. She answers that she will tell you all about it after you tell her about your first day of school. You gladly begin doing so.

Which teenager(s) is/are securely attached and which is/are not? Explain.

Discussions on page 196.

Positive vs. Negative Self – concept

It is also important to remember that a securely attached teenager has a positive self-concept. A teenager with a positive self – concept has strong self-approval.

A teen with a positive self- concept will tend to ...

- like himself, is self-confident and self-assured;
- be happy with life as it is in the here and now;
- not think of himself as being perfect or better than others; he realizes that there is always room for improvement;
- be motivated to do something because he has experienced success;
- be confident in social situations because he gets along will with people;
- allow himself to learn from his mistakes;
- not be afraid to say that he does not know or understand something and ask for help;
- see his environment and himself within his environment realistically;
- seek to move onward and upward in life;
- find healthy playgrounds and playmates with whom to associate;
- have enough self-confidence to cope with new challenges and views them in a positive light.

A teenager with a negative self-concept has weak self- approval.

A teen with a negative self- concept will tend to ...

- be unhappy a lot of the time, or fakes happiness;
- have low self-esteem and low self-refection;
- expect failure in what he does;
- lack motivation because he has not done well in the past;
- look for the easy way out of situations because he lacks self-confidence to work through the situation;
- lack confidence in social situations when meeting new people; sometimes the teen will "fake" having confidence;
- tend to be unaware of the world and life, usually due to a lack of appropriate exposure;
- avoid facing new challenges; he fears failure;

- sometimes set goals that are unrealistically high, and then he feels like a failure when those goals cannot be reached;
- sometimes set goals that are too low, and then he feels little success because the challenge was too easy.

On a special note: Hurt children (*especially teenagers*) are very good Oscar Award winning actors and actresses; Angelina Joelle, Brad Pitt and Tom Cruise, please step aside. Hence, they can appear to be very self-confident. However, if you look very closely and observe over time, you will see their "true colors" emerging. When they are acting, it is as if their lives are a bit too perfect and smooth running. There will also be personal fables spread on top of their life stories.

Do a quick assessment of the teen's self-concept after you have known the teen for a while. You can use the following questions that I compiled over the past few decades, based on clinical observation.

Checklist for a positive self-concept

- Does he seem to have self - confidence? How often and under what circumstances?
- Can he point out specific aspects about himself that he likes, which are realistic?
- Is he able to complete tasks that he sets out to do?
- Is he proud of his name in a non- arrogant way?
- Does he show excitement and curiosity when given the opportunity to try new things?
- Does he set goals that challenge his ability without being impossible to achieve or too simple?
- Does he have realistic dreams and ideas for what he would like to be when he grows up?
- Does he consistently seek out positive peer groups to be a part of?
- Does he know his limitations (*realistically*)?
- Is there a constant, mature caregiver in his life?
- Does he take pride in personal hygiene and appearance?
- Does he respect himself and not fall prey to alluring people he finds sexually attracted?

The more "yes" answers to the above questions, the stronger the self-concept.

Checklist for negative self-concept

- Does he seem to lack self-confidence?
- Does he have trouble saying "realistically" positive things about himself, or does he criticize himself?
- Does he overly compliment himself (*directly or indirectly*)?
- Does he tell personal fables?
- Does he easily become infatuated with people he finds sexually attractive?
- Is he embarrassed by his name; does he give himself a nickname unrelated to his real name?
- Does he seem to change playgrounds and playmates often, and all playgrounds and playmates seem to be unsavory ones?
- Does he get upset when asked to do or try something new because he is afraid of failing or being embarrassed?
- Does he lack realistic dreams and ideas of what he would like to be when he grows up?
- Does he set goals that are unrealistically too high to achieve or too far below is ability?
- Does he have unrealistic dreams and ideas about his future?
- Does he seem not to care about the future?

The more "yes" answers to the above questions, the weaker the self-concept.

Simply put, the unattached teen, with a weak self-concept, will need a mentor.

Self - reflection Questions:

1. Who was your primary caregiver during your early childhood years?
2. How would you describe the level of attachment you had with your primary caregiver?
3. If you believe you did not have a secure base attachment with your primary caregiver, what do you believe was the cause?
4. What personal work have you done to overcome this lack of attachment?

5. Do you believe that you are able to develop healthy, reciprocal relationships with people? Explain.

Diana's Pearls of Wisdom - Usually, it is not until a person has a securely attached relationship to a significant other with whom he feels unconditionally loved and can trust 100% of the time that he has the foundation from which to build healthy, reciprocal relationships with others.

CHAPTER FOUR

What is the Job Description of a Mentor for a Hurt Teen?

What makes a teen hurt?

We've all heard the proverb, "Children learn what they live." I would also like to add – "and in turn will live what they have learned." Well, what have hurt teenagers lived and learned? First of all, they have lived a life of criticism by the significant adult caregivers in their lives, including parents, teachers, coaches, etc. Such significant adults in their lives have called them all of the following and more:

- Lazy
- Stupid
- Bad
- Naughty
- Bad attitude
- Can't act your age
- Never amount to anything
- You are a bad example for your brother, sister, friends, etc.

Why should you be any different? So, when you tell your mentee that he can trust you, you are different, you understand him, and you will not give up on him, don't be offended when he turns a deaf ear, says something sarcastic, appears to not believe you, or pretends to believe you (*hurt teens can be very polite, initially, to strange adults*) then says, "Yeah right" under his breath.

As I mentioned in the last chapter, I must also reiterate that some hurt teenagers have learned to be the quiet, pleasing type; therefore, they never cause any trouble. Such teenagers will not have been called or labeled the aforementioned; however, such teens deeply worry me because they fall between the cracks. Adults and others merely see them as having no troubles; they are just shy. However, such teenagers have a very hollow sense of self and are usually harboring a lot of implosive anger. So, beware of the overly quiet, cooperative teen.

Regardless of the type of hurt teen you work with, I must warn you that if it is your hope to be validated and admired and/or you want to believe that you are saving and rescuing a teen from a terrible life, and he will be forever thankful to you… **CLOSE THIS BOOK NOW AND RETURN IT TO THE BOOKSTORE FOR A REFUND.** You will find such volunteer work as being a reader at a nursing home or caring for abandoned house pets at the animal shelter a far better fit.

On the other hand, if you want to help a teenager become better off because you were a part of his his life than he would be if you had not been a part of his life, then you are on the right path. Oh, I almost forgot, you must also be able to handle feeling taken advantage of at times, being used, perhaps being called ugly and vulgar names and being asked for things. If you feel that you are ready to deal with all of the aforementioned, then welcome aboard the process and keep reading. The rewards will come, albeit far down the line. It is all about delayed gratification, **very delayed gratification**. As I mentioned in the last chapter, it takes 4P's and a teaspoon. In my first book, I mentioned 3P's - patience, persistence and perseverance. I will now add a forth P which is prayer. So… now we have 4P's and a teaspoon. Allow me to also clarify that prayer refers to any means you may have to connect with a transpersonal, higher power that is omnipresent, unconditionally loving and accepting, and (*most importantly*) is available to you 24-7-36-including public holidays.

What is the teaspoon about?

It is about how you measure the progress of your mentee; you do so in teaspoons. You have to be very astute and notice the little accomplishments because the big accomplishments are usually far and few between. A little accomplishment might be a "please" or a "thank you," remembering to write down his homework assignment, asking his friend for permission to barrow his pen before taking it, appreciating your mere presence without having to ask for something, making an appropriate, productive choice on his own or owning his own behavior. When any of the aforementioned or anything similar is said or done, please remember to praise and validate appropriately. Don't be offended if your mentee seems to not respond to praise; this is very often the case. This is the case because praise is very unfamiliar to your mentee. The unfamiliar is always scary and uncomfortable. Continue to praise and validate, within time, your mentee will eventually internalize the praise.

Warning: Be careful; teens will easily become embarrassed if you praise them in public. Please, praise in private.

What is the basic job description for a mentor of a hurt teen?

Simply put, in most cases, the mentor becomes the first adult, significant other in your mentee's life whom he can trust. It is very important to remember that mentors are different from other mental health professionals because they can build an egalitarian relationship that is not bound by the same boundaries and rules of ethics as mental health professionals; although, mentors must also be ethical.

NOTE: The term mental health professional refers to counselors, social workers, probation officers, psychologists or psychiatrists.

Here is the difference...

A mental health professional can only meet the teen in the privacy of his office, the exception being social workers. A mentor is able to be out and about in the community with your mentee.

A mental health professional is only assessable to the teen during the scheduled appointment time. A mentor is available at anytime, if not face-to-face then through e-mail, SMS or phone calls. This doesn't mean that there are not limits and boundaries to the rules of engagement, more on this later.

A mental health professional only makes the teen aware of the options he has for the next step in life and where to look for resources. The mentor actively helps his mentee find the resources and goes out into the field with your mentee to source out the resources. Social workers can also do this.

A mental health professional is highly discouraged, in most cases forbidden, from having dual relationships with clients. A mentor can have a dual relationship as long as it does not impede upon the mentor/mentee relationship. Also, the dual relationship should not impede upon the relationship that the mentor has with other teens and people who are involved in either his life or his mentee's life.

What is meant by dual relationships?

A dual relationship is when someone has more than one relationship with another person, such as when a teacher is also the student's counselor. Another example would be when the wife of the company's CEO is his secretary or a basketball coach is also the student's Boy Scout leader. Some dual relationships are not very likely to cause a conflict of interest or obscure objectivity on behalf of the authority figure, such as a coach who is also the student's Boy Scout leader. On the other hand, a teacher who is also a student's counselor can get very complicated in terms of objectivity.

For example, there would be a conflict of interest if a housemother of a shelter home was also the mentor of one of the teens for whom she cares. This could easily be viewed as the housemother being partial to this one particular teen. Why isn't she also being a mentor for the other 10, 20, 30 or more teens under her care? As we all know, this would be humanly impossible. The same would hold true if the mentor were the teen's teacher or church group leader.

However, as mentioned earlier, there are ethical boundaries and limits to being a mentor for a hurt teenager.

It would be unethical to…

lend money to your mentee; likewise, don't borrow any money from your mentee.

give money to your mentee, other than buying him a meal at Mc Donald's or a drink at a coffee shop. In this case you are not giving money to your mentee; you are treating him. Likewise, don't borrow or take money from your mentee.

lend or give anything to your mentee that you have that they like, even if you no longer want the item. Likewise, don't take anything from your mentee, even if you like it and your mentee truly wants to give it to you.

give gifts; they are already entitled. Give your time. You don't want to quickly become a weekly or monthly personal Santa Clause in your mentee's life. You also don't want a relationship built on material goods. It is about making connection. No gift or amount of money can create genuine connection; connection is totally free and priceless. However, it is OK to give a little something to your mentee for his birthday and Christmas (*or whatever holiday he celebrates*). Also, you **should never** expect a gift in return.

become romantically involved on any level with your mentee or anyone close to your mentee, such as a sibling, aunt or uncle. Also do not become a matchmaker for your mentee, such as introducing him or her to your niece or nephew.

get overly personal about your personal life. Whenever you disclose something about yourself, it should be for your mentee's benefit. If you have had a similar experience, it is OK to be the wounded healer. Again, this must be for the benefit of your mentee. Also, be careful, even if you have had a similar experience, it might not be appropriate to share. This varies from person to person and situation to situation. When in doubt, consult your supervisor.

have too much isolated, private one-on-one time with your mentee. You don't want anything to be your word against his. Yes, many times you want and need privacy due to confidentiality. However, do so at the church, community center or shelter home. This way, you can have the privacy of a room, but others know you are in there. Don't take him to a secluded place in a park.

let a friend of your mentee join you for outings. Even if you are out and about with your mentee and your mentee sees a school friend, don't let him join in the activity. This is your special time with your mentee.

bring your mentee into the privacy of your home or private office at any time for any reason, unless under very unusual circumstances. What would be an unusual circumstance? I can't even think of one. Well......maybe....something like... it is the wee hours of the morning and all department stores are closed. Your mentee rips his pants to the point where they are falling off. You, by coincidence, have a pair that is the exact size in your office. But then.....what would cause you to be out at the wee hours of the morning with your mentee? I guess...under the most unusual circumstances???

WARNING: If you choose to do the following with your mentee, please do so **WITH CAUTION** and be **VERY CLEAR** as to how this is in the best interest of your mentee.

It is recommended that if you include your mentee in family events, please do so with **MUCH CAUTION.** For example, the family is having a large picnic gathering at the beach, and you want to bring your mentee along. It is important to expose hurt teens to functional, healthy family life; however, this puts your mentee at risk for being asked personal questions, or your other family members might not understand the behavior and nature of hurt teens. This could lead to family members becoming GI². Also, your family members might not be aware of confidentiality. If you choose to bring your mentee to the beach with your family, be sure to educate your family members about the nature of hurt teens, what is appropriate to say or ask and the rules of confidentiality. Better yet, give your family members a copy of this book.

Matters of Religion

If any thing about religion comes up, be there for your mentee's religion. Only enlighten your mentee if he seeks to be enlightened. Again, it is **his** religion that you are enlightening, not being a "fisher of men" for your personal religious beliefs. If your mentee is looking for deeper understanding of a certain religion, which you don't know much about or can't relate to, help him find the appropriate person to help him. This is a big part of our jobs as mentors, helping our mentees find the appropriate resources.

Confidentiality

Mentors are obligated to keep confidentiality. Mentors should not discuss with other mentors, friends, family members, teachers or even house mothers what your mentee discloses or any confidential particulars about what you do with your mentee. From the beginning, let your mentee know that if he or she is doing anything that is considered illegal, such as taking drugs, dealing drugs, stealing, skipping school and/or damaging property, you are required by law to report. Also, if he is doing anything that is causing harm to him or to other individuals, you are also obligated to report to the appropriate authorities. This is called informed consent. Informed consent should be about the boundaries and rules of engagement of the mentor/mentee relationship and should be given (*both orally and in writing*) to your mentee and his legal guardian, signed by all parties and agreed upon before the start of the process.

What is considered harmful to self? deliberate self-injury, a secret pregnancy, suicidal thoughts, skipping school, disclosures of abuse or exploitation of any kind, stealing and/or drug involvement.

What is considered harmful to others? plotting to kill or "beat up" someone, egging houses or posting something hurtful about someone on social media, such as a nude picture.

To whom do you report? Report to your mentee's parent, legal guardian or supervisor from the organization, such as the church, school or shelter home. This person will then report to the appropriate authorities. **And yes,** tell your mentee that you are reporting. Assure your mentee that you will be there to support him.

Always remember that a mentor is not ....

- a buddy for your mentee to hang out with and party;
- a person for your mentee to use and become dependent upon;
- an audience for your mentee to live out his false self and personal fables.

What type of teen is a good candidate for having a mentor?

Generally speaking, teenagers who are still in school, not drug or alcohol involved, not involved in criminal behavior and who are interested in having a mentor are good candidates.

What type of teen is not a good candidate for having a mentor?

Teenagers who are presently skipping school, drug involved, in trouble with the law, living on the streets and /or cannot abide by the laws and rules are not good candidates. These teens need a different type of help. If you are fortunate enough to find a teen whose primary caregiver(s) are also motivated to help and understand the mentor program, this is **GREAT**. However, this is very rarely the case.

Having a Mentor's Mentor

It is always advisable to have a mentor's mentor. A mentor's mentor (*which now makes the mentor a mentee*) is a more experienced mentor who can help the novice mentor with his mentee. The mentor's mentor helps the novice mentor double check and clarify ideas about things to do with his mentee. Also the mentor's mentor can help suggest appropriate resources for his mentee. It is also a good idea to have fellow mentors get together and share each other's experiences; please remember to be respectful of confidentiality. No names should be mentioned.

The Driver Situation

Recently, at a monthly meeting with a group of mentors, a situation was disclosed. A mentee disclosed to his mentor that the shelter home van driver was driving a group of boys to a place other than where the shelter home administration thought the driver was driving the boys. Instead the driver was driving the boys to a video arcade to play video games. The mentee who told wasn't one of the boys in the group going to the arcade. One of the boys, among the group of boys going to the arcade, told this mentee. The mentee was afraid to report it. The mentor of the boy who disclosed wanted to know if he should disclose this to the shelter home. I told the mentor that we would go together to the administration of the home and tell what was disclosed. It is then up to the shelter home to properly investigate the situation.

Clearly this needed to be reported and investigated. The driver was breaking the rules of the home and also breaking the law. It did turn out that the story was true. The driver was immediately fired and charges were pressed.

Self-reflective Questions:

1. In 100 words or less describe the essence of a mentor for a hurt teen.
2. What strengths do you believe you will bring to the mentoring process?
3. What do you believe will be a challenge for you?
4. What boundaries will be difficult for you to maintain?
5. Describe the type of teen you believe would be a good match for you, including age, gender, ethnicity, personal issues and circumstances, etc. What makes this a good match?

Diana's Pearls of Wisdom - Helping one is better than helping none. Whenever we help one teen, even in a very small way, it never ends with that one teen. Because that one teen has grown as a result of our help, he will be better able to contribute to society in a positive way and pass on what he has learned to another person in some way; this is the ripple effect. Like when you throw a pebble into the pond, one circle leads to another and to another, and so on.

CHAPTER FIVE

Bandura's Self Efficacy Theory: Can I do it??

Hurt teenagers are teenagers who were hurt children and are now on their way to becoming hurt adults. They will, in-turn, raise hurt children unless the cycle is broken. As children they were not nurtured and taught how to be resilient and properly face adversity. Hence, they were left to themselves to figure out how to deal with adversity. As a result, for the most part, they deal with adversity in a negative, unproductive and harmful way. Generally speaking, when the hurt teen is faced with adversity, he will easily give up or do something self-sabotaging.

Let's compare the following two students:

NOTE: The two case scenarios below are fictitious.

Case of Johnny

Johnny is having trouble in math class. He doesn't understand how to work his math problems. So, instead of asking the teacher for extra help (*because teachers are enemies and he is stupid and lazy and not worth the teacher's time*) he quits trying. He then becomes bored and starts tearing the paper coating off of his crayons and letting the paper fall to the floor. The teacher notices this and yells at Johnny, telling him that he will have to stay inside for recess and clean up the floor. Then as Johnny gets older, he learns how to cheat off of his smart classmates. When the teacher finds out that Johnny cheated, he is suspended from school for three days. Then by the time Johnny is 16, he drops out of high school and has become totally unmotivated by the whole academic scene. In short, Johnny is a hurt teen.

Case of Mary

Mary is having trouble in math class. So... she raises her hand and asks the teacher to please go over the problem again. When Mary goes home and begins to do her homework, she realizes that she is confused, once again, about how to work the problems. Her mother (*who is pretty good in math*) is not yet home from work. Mary calls her friend and asks if they can get together and work on the problems. In class the next day, Mary asks the teacher if she is doing the problems correctly. Mary continues to have difficulties in math throughout high school; it is the one subject that she just doesn't seem to understand (*neither do I*). She has decided to major in philosophy; hopefully, she won't have to take more than one or two basic math classes during her university career.

When facing a challenge, Johnny does not believe that he can do well in school, so he quits. He is not motivated to try or get help. It can be said that Johnny has low self-efficacy. On the other hand, Mary believes that she can do well; therefore, she is willing to try and look for assistance. It can be said that Mary has high self-efficacy.

Note: Self – efficacy does not only pertain to academics.

What is Self-efficacy?

Self - efficacy is Alfred Bandura's (born in1925) social learning theory, which explains that a person's attitudes, abilities, and cognitive skills comprise what is known as his self-system. This system plays a major role in how a person perceives situations and how he behaves in response to different situations. Bandura calls this self-system, self-efficacy. It is your belief in your own abilities to deal with various situations. This belief system plays a very important role in not only how you feel about yourself but also plays an important roll in whether or not you successfully achieve your goals in life. Self-efficacy is also closely intertwined with a person's sense of self-esteem. Furthermore, according to Bandura, self-efficacy is the belief in one's capabilities to organize and execute the courses of actions required to manage prospective situations.

In other words, self-efficacy is a person's belief in his ability to accomplish tasks or succeed in a particular situation. Bandura described these beliefs as determinants of how people think, behave, and feel.

Ever since Bandura introduced his theory in 1977, self-efficacy has become known to impact many aspects of humans' emotional experiences, such as psychological states, behavior, reactions to situations and motivation.

Bandura, A. (1995). *Self-Efficacy in Changing Societies*. Cambridge University Press.

The Role of Self-efficacy in a Person's Life

Most people can identify goals they want to accomplish, things they would like to change and things they would like to achieve. This is the easy part. Likewise, most people also find that putting these goals and plans into action is much easier said than done. Bandura's self-efficacy theory is centered around how an individual's self-efficacy plays a major role in how goals, tasks, and challenges are approached, executed, carried through or not carried through.

How do we know if a person has a strong sense of self-efficacy?

Based on my clinical experience, I have come to know that people with a strong sense of self-efficacy...

- are not afraid of challenging problems; they are happy to take on the challenge, jump in and try;
- develop deeper interests in the activities in which they participate;
- form a stronger sense of commitment to their interests and activities;
- recover quickly from setbacks and disappointments;
- do not expect to be perfect all the time.

Based on my clinical experience, I have come to know that people with a weak sense of self-efficacy ...

- avoid challenging tasks;
- are quick to appoint others to do tasks they do not believe they can do;

- are very willing to "piggy back" on the work of others and get their share of the credit;
- believe that difficult tasks and situations are beyond their capabilities;
- focus on personal failings and negative outcomes;
- quickly lose confidence in personal abilities.

Notice, that self-efficacy very much parallels with self-esteem and self-concept.

Sources of Self-efficacy

Where does self-efficacy come from? How does self-efficacy develop?

Well... self-efficacy is not one of those things that is passed through DNA. It cannot be received as a gift on your birthday; you can't barrow it from friends (*or enemies for that matter*); it cannot be bought on sale at the nearest department store, grown on organic farm, nor can it be manufactured in a lab. A person begins to develop his sense of self-efficacy during his early childhood years and continues to develop self-efficacy throughout his lifespan. As a young toddler begins to explore and discover his environment, he learns to accomplish simple tasks and situations. These accomplishments make him feel autonomous and capable. This begins his journey of building a sense of strong self-efficacy.

This continues as he grows and develops. The young child continues to acquire new skills, experiences, understanding and achievement. All the while, the significant adults in his life are consistently validating and encouraging him along the way. This is what cultivates strong self-efficacy. The more positive and successful the person's achievements are, the stronger his sense of self-efficacy will be. If the child experiences more failures or negative experiences, he will develop a weak sense of self-efficacy. In short, the more the positive outweighs the negative the stronger the person's sense of self-efficacy. It is that simple.

According to Bandura, there are four aspects a person must consistently have in order to develop a strong sense of self-efficacy.

1. Mastery Experiences

Mastery experiences simply means that the person experiences success as he tries to do something. This strengthens his belief in his capabilities and motivates him to want to continue trying. This leads to strong self-efficacy. On the other hand, if the person experiences failure or continuously has to struggle to do something, he will become discouraged and not be motivated to try. This is the reason that it is so important to accentuate the positive in terms of someone's efforts. Don't dwell on the 60 % or so that is wrong, celebrate the 40% that is correct. Then encourage him to think of what he can do to bring his work to the next level.

2. Social Modeling

Observing other people of equal ability successfully completing a task is another important source of building strong self-efficacy. According to Bandura, when we see another person succeed through hard work and effort, we are motivated to try harder. Like… if he can do it; I can do it. Don't forget the other person must be of **EQUAL ABILITY**, which doesn't necessarily mean the same age. A beginning golf player will be motivated if another beginner scores a hole in one. On the other hand, if the same beginner sees Tiger Woods score a hole in one, this would not be social modeling because needless to say, Tiger Woods is not of equal ability as the beginner. However, Tiger Woods can serve as an inspiration.

3. Social Persuasion

Bandura also believed that it is important for people to get encouragement from significant others in order to be motivated to try and succeed. Through positive validation and encouragement from others, especially significant others, a person will become motivated to achieve a goal. Verbal encouragement from other people helps us to overcome self-doubt and helps give us the fortitude to continue to try.

It is important that the encouragement is realistic and genuinely sincere. In other words, we need to make sure that we are encouraging someone to try a task that is within their realm of capability. It won't be realistic to ask a person who has only been ice-skating for a year to "try out" for the Olympic team. Of course, this sounds so obvious; however, you would be surprised by how many parents, teachers, coaches and leaders have encouraged teens to try for something that is out of their league. This is very counterproductive and does not enhance self-efficacy. Another very important thing to consider is whether or not the person even wants to succeed in whatever it is we are encouraging him to do. A big part of accomplishing something is the intrinsic motivation one has to succeed in the first place.

4. Psychological Responses

In developing a strong sense of self-efficacy, Bandura believed that it is important not to become our own worse enemy. Our own responses and emotional reactions to situations also play an important role in self-efficacy. Moods, emotional states, physical reactions, and stress levels can all impact how we feel about our personal abilities in a particular situation. A person who becomes extremely nervous before speaking in public may develop a weak sense of self-efficacy in these situations. By learning how to minimize stress and elevate our mood when facing difficult or challenging tasks, we can improve our sense of self-efficacy.

Bandura, A. (1977). *Self-efficacy: Toward a unifying theory of behavioral change.* Psychological Review, 84, 191-215

Overall Self-efficacy vs. Self-efficacy related to certain tasks

It is important to remember that we all have an overall sense of self-efficacy and a sense of self- efficacy as related to certain skills. A high functioning, successful person will have high self-efficacy; however, perhaps the same person might have low self-efficacy when it comes to dancing because he isn't very coordinated and hasn't experienced success when trying to learn dances in the past. Therefore, the person doesn't believe he will ever learn to dance and avoids even trying to learn to dance. It could be said that this person has low self-efficacy when it comes to dancing.

We all have low self-efficacy when it comes to some certain task. Mine, for example, is cooking; I burn water, no kidding. What is important is one's overall sense of self- efficacy. When a person has high overall self-efficacy, it doesn't matter that in a few areas the person has low self-efficacy. The person will still be willing and open to trying to learn new things. On the other hand, when a person has low overall self-efficacy, he is not inclined to try to learn and explore new things. Generally speaking, hurt teenagers have low self-efficacy and tend to avoid new experiences, which they believe will be challenging; hence, a big part of our work as mentors is to enhance our mentees' levels of self-efficacy.

Self-reflective Questions:

1. Evaluate your level of self-efficacy today? What contributes to this in terms of the four aspects?
2. Think back to when you were a teen. What was your level of self-efficacy? What factors contributed to your level of self-efficacy as a teen in terms of the four aspects?

Diana's Pearls of Wisdom – It's not the weight and size of the load that weighs us down, it's how we choose to carry it. It is easier to carry a big, heavy bag by placing it in a wagon and pulling the wagon than it would be to throw the bag over our shoulder and carry it. Likewise, when we are aware of our strengths and limitations, prioritize our tasks, and get appropriate help and assistance, our load is much easier to carry.

CHAPTER SIX

James Marcia: Ego Identity States

It's important, as a mentor of hurt teens, to understand Marcia's theory of ego identity states because a big part of helping hurt teens is to help them explore and discover their interests, talents and proclivities based upon who they authentically are. It is important for everyone to be in touch with who he is before he can make decisions about post-secondary education or job and career choices in his best interest.

James Marcia - Ego States

James Marcia (1902 – 1994) was an American developmental psychologist, who specialized in adolescent development. He was a disciple of Eric Erickson. Marcia explained the adolescent years as being a time of developing an identity status. This of course goes hand-in-hand with developing a true, realistic sense of self. Marcia further defines the adolescent years as living through a "crisis" and finally making a commitment by the age of 18. This is usually around the time a teenager graduates from secondary school. At which point, life is never the same.

Marcia, J. et al. (1993). *Ego Identity: – A Handbook for Psychosocial Research.* **Springer Verlag Publishers, New York, NY.**

I don't like to think of this time of confusion as a "crisis." This seems to me (*I am only speaking for myself*) to be too strong of a word. I rather think of the "confusion" as a time of exploring and discovering. Actually, exploring and discovering one's interests, talents and proclivities begins at birth. However, it continues through the lifespan. What makes the end of the teenage years so important in this process is that upon high school graduation, the older teen will make a choice about his next step in life. Will he choose higher education, job skill training, finding a job or a combination of both? Parents and caregivers are very important agents during this stage of exploring and discovering, hopefully for the better. All too often parents get all "'uptight" because the teen can't stick to one activity and commit. Well…he is exploring and discovering. Some parents are too determined to have their teens excel at certain hobbies and activities, some to the extent of vicarious living. Coaches and other significant adults can also live vicariously through their team members or students… **BEWARE.** Vicarious living is usually unconscious on the part of the parent, coach or significant adult.

What is vicarious living?

Simply put, it is living your life dreams and wishes through another person's life. It is so sad that children are forced to take piano lessons, play certain sports, or take ballet lessons when they despise the activity; however, they will endure it because it is their parents' unlived dream. Well, Mom and Dad, it is never too late; there are even pianos in the old folks' homes. Watch the reality show, *Toddlers and Tiaras*. This is vicarious living to the max.

I will share my own story as a parent. My son, Raymond, who is now an adult, has spent his whole life dancing. He tried soccer when he was six but came home from practice one day and told me he would rather take dance lessons. I said sure, great, let's do it. I also grew up dancing and even taught dance as an adult. My brother was a professional ballet dancer for many years. Yes, I really hoped Raymond would also dance professionally. Perhaps not classical ballet because he has always preferred modern dance and tap, but I have always thought that Las Vegas or a cruise ship would be a great way for him to dance on stage and get paid.

When he entered university, he decided to major in psychology and child advocacy and minor in dance performance. Then during his third year of university, he called one night and told me he was joining the Army National Guard. I thought, **what in the world!!!** Immediately, visions of Colonel Clank and Gomer Pyle raced through my head. For those of you who are "experienced" enough (*notice that I didn't say old enough*) to remember these comical characters, you know what I mean. If you haven't been among the living long enough to know these comical characters, just imagine Lady Gaga playing on a major league American football team, and you'll get the picture. I mean… Raymond just isn't military material. He is one of these highly right-brained creative types and the more out of the box, the better. Isn't this the antithesis of military protocol?

Well… much to my surprise, as he became involved in Army life, I quickly saw that it gave him a sense of brotherhood, and yes, there are opportunities for creative expression in the Army. Furthermore, the "by the book" organization of the military gives his impulsive, haphazard organization style (*he takes after his mother*) some grounded structure. In short, the Army has been a very positive experience for Raymond. As the story goes, Raymond is now studying to become a clinical psychologist and hopes to work with soliders suffering form PTSD. He still takes dance classes on a regular basis and is considering exploring dance therapy as a second profession.

What is most important is that Raymond is doing what **HE** wants to do. It is his decision what role dance will play in his life. As for seeing him dance professionally… maybe one day. On the other hand, if the day never comes, this is perfectly fine. Meanwhile, he can jete' and shuffle- ball-change across the battlefield.

Marcia's Four Identity Statuses are as follows:

Identity Status is a term that Marcia coined to name the four different ego states of self-awareness.

1. Identity Achievement – An older teen who has attained identity achievement, has made a post-secondary school life decision based upon realistic self- awareness. He has spent his teenage years exploring different activities and has decided for himself which ones he is interested in and which ones he isn't. As a result, he is able to choose his post-secondary school life path based on his interests, talents and proclivities.

2. Foreclosure – An older teen in a state of foreclosure has made a post-secondary life decision based upon the wishes of someone else, doing what his friends are doing or doing what is convenient. The teen has not spent time exploring different options and deciding for himself what he is interested in doing. He has not considered what would be a good fit for him. Generally speaking, teens in foreclosure usually do not have a strong sense of self.

3. Moratorium – The older teen is still exploring. He needs more time to explore his interests, talents and proclivities.

4. Identity Diffusion - An older teen, who is in a state of identity diffusion, has an absence of commitment and a lack of serious consideration of alternatives. He is not interested in making choices about his future. In short, he doesn't care.

Marcia, J. et al. (1993). *Ego Identity: A Handbook for Psychosocial Research.* Springer – Verlag Publishers, New York, NY.

Activity- Let's Explore

Below are 12 teenagers. All 12 are 18-years old, and they are in their final semester of secondary school. In which ego identity state is each teenager? A few are somewhat debatable.

Discussion on page 196 – No peeping, please.

NOTE: All of the following case scenarios are fictitious.

Ricky has been very active during his high school years. He has participated in several sports, the drama club, the marine science club, and he has been a member of the honor society every year. He also loves to work on racing car engines. His uncle owns an automobile mechanics shop, and Ricky has been helping his uncle on weekends ever since he was 12. Ricky has decided to take a gap year before starting his first year of university. He isn't sure what he wants to study at university, so he will take general studies courses his first year. Rick plans to spend his gap year working at his uncle's shop, traveling and being a volunteer tutor for disadvantaged children.

Alice has lived in the same small, rural community all of her life. Her family has owned and run a diner for the past four generations. Alice and her three siblings have been working in the family business throughout their high school years. Alice has been dating her childhood sweetheart, Jack, for the past three years. Jack has decided to join the Army and will spend the next three months in basic training in another state. They hope to stay together and get married someday. Sometimes, Alice dreams of attending a university in a big city. She would be the first in her family to attend college, but for now it is important to help out in the family business.

Tara is a talented and dedicated ice-skater. She has been skating since the age of five and has won gold medals in several competitions. Her coach believes that she has the potential to be chosen for the Olympic team. Tara has been homeschooled all of her life. Practicing ice-skating four to six hours a day doesn't leave time for traditional schooling. She has done very well with her on-line homeschooling curriculum and is graduating with a 4.0 average. Math and social studies have been her favorite subjects. Now that she has graduated, she will continue her education by taking some on-line college courses while she trains for the Olympics. She will also help teach young children how to ice skate two evenings a week.

Roger has just finished night school at the age of 19. He dropped out of high school at 15 and got mixed up with the wrong crowd. He was arrested and sent to the juvenile detention center when he was 16 for stealing cars. He was released and put on probation after eighteen months. Roger has also been in drug rehab twice for cocaine addiction. He has been drug free for the past year. Roger is currently on probation. His probation officer says that he is doing well. Next week he will begin taking classes to become a CNA (Certified Nurse's Assistant). Roger will also work at a gas station part-time to earn money. He has joined a church, and his pastor is letting him stay at his house until he can finish trade school and save enough money to get a place of his own. Roger is hoping to meet some new friends.

Lily is the youngest of six children. Her mother has been a single, working mother all of her life. Her father has been in jail for murder; it was a drug deal that went wrong. All of her siblings are married with children. She has so many nieces and nephews that she looses count. Lily used to baby sit a lot for them when she first started secondary school; however, for the past two years, she finally began to say, no. She made up her mind to go to nursing school two years ago when her school had a career day and a nurse came to give a speech. Lily's favorite subject in high school is biology. Her school counselor even arranged for her to go visit the vocational school that offers a nursing program. Lily can finish the program in two years. She will then go to work and start saving money to complete her RN (Registered Nurse) degree.

Billy was a very active high school student. He was the president of the student council, stage manager for the theater group and captain of the softball team. He has thought about majoring in sports medicine, but he also likes graphic arts. This coming semester he will take a couple of core curriculum courses at the community college and coach little league soft ball.

Sabrina is a girl of the streets. She was born to drug addicted parents and was taken away from her parents by authorities due to physical abuse and neglect. Her parents were forced to terminate parental rights when she was six. She hasn't seen her birth parents since she was five; she doesn't even know if they are still alive. Sabrina is so glad to finally be out of foster care this month. She is sooooo sick of adult caregivers making and breaking promises. It seems like all foster parents want is the state check they get each month for fostering her. Sabrina is not sure what her future holds. One of her friends, who lives with her boyfriend, has invited Sabrina to live with them. This should be OK. The boyfriend uses cocaine, but Sabrina knows to stay away from it. Eventually she will look for a job, but for now she just needs to get out of the foster care system and live her life.

Rob will graduate this weekend. He did OK in school. He managed to pass all of his courses. The only extra-curricular activity he participated in was the ecology club. He has always been fascinated by nature and protecting the environment. Rob always liked to help his parents mow the lawn and tend to the garden since the age of five. When he was 13, he noticed that a new family moved in down the street and their grass was very high. Rob went to the neighbor's house, rang their doorbell and asked if he could mow their lawn for 20 dollars. The family was very happy to have Rob's help. He has been mowing this family's lawn, as well as the lawns of many other families, ever since. Over the past year, Rob has been working with a small business consultant and a financial planner to make his lawn business an official business. Last week he rented a small office space and hired three lawn assistants and one secretary. Last year he made a profit of 10,000 dollars. This year his goal is to make a profit of 15,000 dollars after taxes and business expenses.

Sally has been raised in an aristocratic family. Her family has lived in the same city for the past seven generations. She is the descendant of wealthy factory owners who manufacture chemical products. Sally attended a private school for girls. Most of her classmates are going to university. Sally never was interested in higher education; she is fortunate to be independently wealthy. Sally would rather learn vicariously by living her life day-to-day and see what comes her way.

Stephen is the fifth child of 10 children. His family members are very devout fundamental Christians. All 10 children have been homeschooled. Stephen has been very active in the church's youth group, but he has not socialized outside of his family and church community. Now that Stephen has completed his correspondence high school diploma, he will begin working as an assistant to the church's secretary. He enjoys the atmosphere of the church and is looking forward to working for the church. His girlfriend, Sally, who was also homeschooled, will also begin working for the church. Stephen is not sure whether or not he is interested in college. He has thought about going to a Bible college and getting a degree in youth ministry; he knows that he wants to work in a church setting. However, for now he is looking forward to going to work and making his own money. Stephen will keep praying about his life and let God decide the rest.

Lucy is from a low socio-economic family. She is an only child being raised by a single mother. Her mother was very supportive of her education and insisted that Lucy stay in school until she graduated from high school. Her mother works as a nursing assistant at the community's old folks home. Lucy did well in school and even managed to stay away from the many negative peer influences. Lucy has a job washing hair at a hair salon in her neighborhood. It isn't her favorite thing, but it helps her hard working mother pay the bills. Lucy has always dreamed of being an airline stewardess. Being able to travel to different places around the world sounds so exciting. Her high school counselor gave her the training requirements and information from a few different airlines. Lucy is not ready to make the call. She hasn't even told her mom about her wishes, yet. Also, Lucy likes the idea of working with animals. She did a volunteer project at the animal shelter as an assignment for her biology class. She has always loved domestic animals; unfortunately, her mother won't let her have a pet because they can't afford to feed a pet.

Daniel is from a very prominent family. His father is a fourth generation lawyer and is presently the district attorney for his town. Daniel has spent many days going to his Dad's office and observing trials in the courtroom. Daniel was an excellent high school student; he graduated valedictorian of his class. He has been accepted into law school, his Dad's alma mater. Daniel will work hard over the next six years; after which, he will work in his father's law firm.

Discussion on Page 196

Notice: Marcia's theory very much parallels with Erickson's 5th stage of psychosocial development.

It is also important to keep in mind that Marcia was not making the point that an 18 - year old should know what he wants to do for the rest of his life. Many adults go through career and job changes, as well as embark upon second careers, throughout their adult lives. As I understand it, having reached a stage of identity achievement merely means that the older teen has made a decision about his first step toward adult life, education, job and career choices based on his interests, talents and proclivities.

Self - reflective Questions:

1. What stage of ego development were you in when you finished secondary school?
2. What about your upbringing and life experiences brought you to that stage?
3. How do you see yourself helping your mentee develop identity achievement? What activities and resources will you expose him to?

Let's Go Deeper...

What do you see as the relationship between parenting styles and identity status; which parenting and leadership styles are likely to promote the different identity statuses? See Chapter 8 for parenting, mentoring and leadership styles.

Diana's Pearls of Wisdom – It is through exposure and having opportunities to explore that we begin to tap into our innate interests, talents and proclivities.

CHAPTER SEVEN

Discovering Interests, Talents and Proclivities

Before we can begin to help hurt teens with building a true sense of self and all of the components involved, such as personal resources, self-efficacy and identity achievement, we must first help the hurt teen discover his talents, interests and proclivities. Hurt teenagers do not know what to do after high school because they usually have no idea about their interests, talents and proclivities. Not knowing one's interests, talents and proclivities (*realistically I must add*) is a sign of a weak sense of self. Most people understand what I mean by interests and talents. However, several people ask me what I mean by proclivities.

What are proclivities?

The Merriam- Webster Dictionary defines proclivities as "a strong inherent inclination toward something."

Merriam- Webster Dictionary, **Encyclopedia Britannica, Inc., Pittsburg, PA. (2009)**

More directly said, proclivities are activities that we have a fascination for, want to engage in often, enjoy and want to learn more about. It is very easy to spot the proclivities of preschoolers. Imagine a preschooler you know; what does he do in his spare time without being asked? Does he build things with Lego blocks, dance around the room, play soccer, sit behind a piano and make up tunes, doodle or pretend to cook? Whatever he does, time and again without being told, is a proclivity. It is during our preschool years that we are fortunate enough to have the time to indulge ourselves in our proclivities because these are the years that most of us have non-directed free time. Once we enter formal schooling, our free time is taken up with homework, organized after school activities and perhaps house chores, among other things.

Now, sorry folks, computer games and gadgets are not proclivities, unless we are programing them, making up new software, or creating new games. Just sitting down for hours playing video games, non-stop, is an addiction not a proclivity.

Hurt teenagers are usually not in touch with their proclivities because, unlike unhurt teenagers, they have not had the opportunity to explore and discover different activities. Also, even the fortunate ones who discover their proclivities, don't always know how to capitalize on them. Some hurt teenagers will be in touch with their proclivities. This is great; please help them begin to capitalize on their proclivities. For the hurt teens, who are not aware of their proclivities, helping them discover their proclivities is an essential part of mentoring. Higher education, job training and/or career success, on any level, is going to be based on understanding and exercising our talents, interests and proclivities. It is a shame when someone stays in a job or career his whole life that doesn't allow him to exercise his talents, interests and proclivities. Where does the mentor begin in helping his teen discover his proclivities? Well, I don't recommend asking him, "What do you like to do other than play computer games?" You need to become a Pink Panther and investigate.

How to Be a Pink Panther

1. Be aware of the types of movies and books your mentee reads and watches just because he wants to read or watch them. The characters a person likes in books and movies reveal something about the person. I will recommend an expressive arts project about movie and book characters in Chapter 15.
2. Be aware of what they talk about with other teenagers, such as music, sports, dance, art, etc.
3. What does your mentee like to do and talk about during your sessions together?
4. When your mentee discovers something that interests him, help him find opportunities to explore the interest. This can be done either

through hands on participation or talking with people who have experience with this particular activity.

5. **EXPOSURE – EXPOSURE – EXPOSURE** – please give your mentee as many opportunities as possible to be exposed to different events, such as theatre plays and music concerts. Also, give him as many opportunities as possible to participate in different activities, such as sports, music, dance or art. The more opportunities you give your mentee, the better.

Extra-curricular activities are just as important as reading, writing and arithmetic.

It drives me crazy (*I know it is a short drive*) when students are ban from extra-curricular activities because their grades are low, or they are failing subjects. I can understand the importance of grades; however, especially when it comes to hurt teens who need to build a sense of self, extra-curricular activities are more important than reading and writing. When hurt teens become interested in an activity, it can become their lifeline... really. I can tell you uncountable (*literally uncountable*) stories of hurt teenagers who one day discovered they had an interest in either dance, art, sports, cooking, rebuilding car engines, etc. and suddenly they had a reason to stay in school, get passing grades and graduate. Extra-curricular activities can be great for building and enhancing self-esteem. As I have preached all along, hurt teens have low self-esteem.

Academics vs. Extra-curricular activities: So, what is the difference?

Ideally, academics enhance the teen's cognitive, social, emotional, creative and physical growth; however, the emphasis is on cognitive growth. Also academics are evaluated, hence with academics comes the stigma of pass, fail, correct, incorrect, good, bad, etc. Not that this is bad.

After all, this has been the age-old purpose of the schooling and learning process. For the hurt teen, who already feels "not good enough" academics can become one more reminder to him that he "is not good enough." On the other hand, extra-curricular activities also enhance the child's cognitive, social, emotional, creative and physical growth. However, the emphasis is on social and emotional growth... at least it should be. Usually, the concept of pass, fail, right or wrong isn't associated with extra-curricular activities. I realize that some sports can be very competitive and have the win or loose stigma to them. If this is the case, it might not be a good fit for a hurt teen. On the other hand, if the hurt teen likes the sport, is there by choice and is OK with the competitive nature, then this is OK.

As has been mentioned, hurt teens need opportunities to "choose." Extra-curricular activities is a great opportunity for the teen to choose what he wants to do. No teen gets to choose whether or not he takes, math, science or English; however, he does get to choose his extra-curricular activities. **LET HIM CHOOSE**. Extra-curricular activities will quickly loose there potential to be self-esteem enhancers if the teen is forced to participate.

So, which is more important academics or extra-curricular activities?

If you are asking me *(if not, please let me tell you anyway)*, they are equally important, especially in the life of a hurt teen. When I train shelter home caregivers *(shelter homes are full of hurt teens)* one of the first questions I ask is "What about your teens irritate you the most?" One of the most popular answers that comes up time and again is "They don't care about school; don't they know that education is the key to success in life? Don't they know that they will never get into university without good grades, etc...." Then I hear about all the things shelter home parents do for their teens to help then get a "good" education. They help them with their homework, bribe them to do their homework, hire tutors, etc.

WOW...this is really putting the cart before the horse. To care about academic achievement, one must first care about himself. Hurt teens haven't developed self-care, as of yet, so this is the pan ultimate goal of a mentor. The mentor helps his mentee cultivate a self-care system. Also, teachers and school administrators can quickly pour gasoline on a fire that is already roaring and blazing by telling the hurt teen that he is lazy, a troublemaker, doesn't act his age, you are suspended, you are being sent to detention, etc. Why should the teen care about school and academics?

To summarize the psychology of academic achievement in a nutshell, think of it this way. It takes high self-esteem to excel in academics. Again, hurt teenagers will have to first enhance their levels of self-esteem. Before self-esteem can be enhanced, a sense of unconditional love and belonging must be felt by the hurt teen. **GO FOR IT MENTORS**. Then, and only then, academics will become more important. If extracurricular activities are helping the hurt teen enhance his self- esteem, please don't take them away. **Thank you very much.**

One other thing, don't be bothered if the teen changes the activity every semester, he is exploring. This is what we want him to do. We want him to **EXPLORE AND DISCOVER** his talents, interests and proclivities. Let's think about it - is all of this extra tutoring and homework coaching (*which usually needs to be paid for*) really helping? If it is, great, continue. If not, why continue with it? It's sort of like hoping someone who hates spinach will begin to like it more if we feed him more spinach.

So, now you want to ask me, "So, what do I do to get him to like math, science, English, etc. and pass." There are no magic wands to wave. If I had such a wand, I would be a billionaire. We must first work on connection and relationship; this in-turn will help build your hurt teenager's self-esteem. The higher his self- esteem, the better his self-care system will be. The better his self-care system, the more positive his attitude will be toward academics within time. **Let's put the horse before the cart, please…Thank You.**

Self – reflective Questions:

1. What are your talents, interests and proclivities?
2. When you were a teenager, how did you go about exploring and discovering your talents, interests and proclivities?
3. Who were the significant people who helped you to discover your talents, interests and proclivities?
4. Based on the ideas given above, which activities do you believe you will find must helpful in helping your mentee discover his talents, interests and proclivities?
5. Come up with some better ideas of your own to help your mentee discover his talents, interests and proclivities.

Diana's Pearls of Wisdom – Never…. I repeat, Never….one more time, **NEVER** take away an activity that the teen really enjoys and gives him a sense of pride and accomplishment. Only a GI^2 would do such a thing.

CHAPTER EIGHT

Parenting, Leadership and Mentoring Styles

My mentoring styles are the same as my parenting styles, which are the same as leadership styles; parents and mentors are also leadership roles. I will once again introduce (*from my first book*) my parenting styles; however, in this book we will think of them not only as parenting styles but also as mentoring and leadership styles. As you read this chapter, continue to think about what leadership style you tend to exercise. You will probably see yourself in certain aspects of different styles at different times in different situations, but you will also see that you have a dominant style as well.

Simply said, a leadership style is a way in which a leader goes about interacting with the people he leads. As a result of his leadership style, a certain type of rapport is built between the leader and the person or people whom he is leading.

The following leadership styles are based on the research and theory of Diane Braumrind's parenting styles. Braumrind only worked with and researched parents of preschoolers back in the 1960's. I have taken the liberty to expand upon Braumrind's three parenting styles by adding two new styles and giving new names to Braumrind's three original styles. Furthermore, these five styles do not only pertain to parenting preschoolers, but to parenting and/or leading people of all ages in all types of situations. It is also important to remember that leadership styles tend to be transgenerational. In short, people will lead the way that they have been led. Also, the way a person leads is based on the way he was parented. In short, parenting and leadership styles are synonymous.

Please note that these five styles describe any type of leader, such as teacher, boss, mentor, coach, etc.

The five styles of leadership are dictator, doormat, bonded, ghost and dictating ghost. It is important to always remember that all five leadership styles can be found in all places of the world and within all socio-economic classes. Certain cultures may have more of one style than another; however, all five styles can be found everywhere.

Again, leadership styles are ways in which a leader interacts and communicates both verbally and non- verbally; this allows for a certain type of rapport to be established between the leader and the person or people he is leading. Just as the style of parenting a parent uses with a child has a great barring on how the child will grow in self-concept and self-efficacy, the leadership style a leader uses with the person he is leading has a great impact on the person's self-concept, self-esteem and self-efficacy. I repeat, all of the leadership styles can be found in all walks of life in all parts of the world. By "world" I mean planet Earth; I am not sure what goes on in outer space. As mentioned earlier, I will research the cosmos in my next life. Planet Earth is keeping me busy enough during this lifetime.

Diana's Five Leadership Styles

There are five leadership styles: dictating, bonded, doormat, ghost and dictating ghost. First, I will explain the styles from a parenting point of view then I will discuss the types from a leadership/mentor point of view.

Dictating Parenting Style... It's my way or the highway.

Dictating parents are control freaks. Such parents try to run the child's life for him. They don't trust the child to be able to make appropriate choices or decisions. They have certain ideas about specific ways they want their children to grow up. Dictating parents have a tendency to use external controls, such as criticism, yelling, and belittling or even corporal punishment. The dictating parent also tends to focus on the negative, what is wrong and what needs to be better, as opposed to what is right and good. The child, generally speaking, is not given the opportunity to make his own appropriate choices and decisions.

As a result, the child usually has low self-esteem or an unrealistic inflated sense of self, which is actually serving to mask his insecurities. When faced with having to make a decision, such children usually don't know how. Dictating parents truly believe that they are doing what is best for their children, molding them into the "right" type of people. Well...what can I say....GI[2].

Children and teenagers of dictating parents tend to...

- be either quiet, compliant and pleasing or anxious and unhappy. The quiet, compliant and pleasing type is trying to avoid criticism or punishment. The anxious and unhappy type will have a tendency to turn rebellious, especially in their teenage years;
- have a hard time making simple age appropriate decisions, such as choosing the best summer camp program to attend;
- have low self-esteem and self-doubt;
- strive to be overachievers. They feel if they are perfect, they will finally please Mom and Dad;
- be at risk for substance abuse, eating disorders and other addictions;
- believe that they are better than others and have a superiority complex;
- sometimes, grow up in a state of ignorant bliss, believing that they are true to themselves and Mom and Dad really do make the best choices for them.

Dictating Parents of Upper and Middle Class

Dictating parents of upper and middle class truly believe that they are doing what is best for their child, and they are going out of their way and making tremendous sacrifices to give their children the best opportunities. Dictating parents tend to be competitive. They worry about what the neighbors think; they want their children to be better than the neighbor's children. They are also very concerned about the family's reputation and standing in the community. They often get paranoid and become pink panthers, snooping into their children's business. Upper and middle class dictating parents can sometimes live their lives vicariously through their children. They are hoping (*in some cases even insisting*) that their children will live their unfulfilled dreams. They may also have a tendency to make up personal fables about their children.

Dictating Parents of Lower Class and Poverty

Dictating parents of lower class and poverty tend to be overly concerned with protecting their children from the woes of the environment, such as drugs, drive by shootings, skipping school, etc. They want their children to stay out of trouble and get an education; however they do not necessarily want them to leave the neighborhood. They want their children to be able to help the family (*sometimes extended family members as well*) by getting a job as soon as possible and help with the finances. Lower and poverty class children of dictating parents also, at times, become parentified children. An example of a parentified child would be a 13-year-old girl who is expected to come home from school everyday and help her younger siblings with their homework, cook dinner for them and put them to bed.

The Psyche of the Dictating Parent

The dictating parent is usually the product of dictating parents; hence he has insecurities and self-doubts as well. Now is the time that he can feel in control and important by bossing his children around; this is another example of transgenerational dysfunction. This will continue until someone breaks the cycle.

Dictating Leadership Style

Like the dictating parent, dictating leaders are also control freaks. They have an attitude of "I am the expert; therefore, I know what is best. Do it my way and no questions asked." Dictating leaders are low in connection and involvement. The leader listens very little to the people under his leadership. The dictating leader does not take the unique individual person's proclivities, interests and talents into account. They often have external measures of control, such as criticisms, belittling, docking pay, etc. The negative is always commented upon, and the positive is overlooked. The follower has very little opportunity to make choices. As a result, the follower has either low self-confidence or an overly inflated ego (*which is usually a cover for low self-esteem*).

Followers of dictating leaders, usually...

- don't feel a sense of autonomy in their project;
- never validate themselves because they are concentrating on improving their weaknesses to please the boss instead of celebrating their strengths;
- lack problem solving skills because problems are solved for them;
- do not know how to make original contributions to the project because they are never given the chance;
- don't have the opportunity to tap into their unique skills.

Like the child in a state of ignorant bliss, the follower can also find comfort in such working conditions and feel content.

What is the inner psyche of the dictating leader?

Dictating leaders usually have a low sense of self-confidence. They are overly concerned about being in control. The thought of loosing control makes them very anxious. They have a very ridged mindset on how their followers should work, behave, think and believe. Dictators tend to be overly concerned about loosing face in the eyes of their bosses. They have a tendency to always compare people to other people. Like the dictating parent, the dictating leader can also have aspects of vicarious living. He expects his followers to live out his unfulfilled dreams. For example, the coach that wants his team to win the state championship because his team never did.

Doormat Parenting Style.... Well, I guess you can.

Doormat parents do not know how to set appropriate boundaries and limits with their children. Doormat parents are afraid to upset their children. Doormats hate disharmony and are looking for acceptance and approval; this is because they didn't get it growing up. They are the pleasing type. The child of doormat parents quickly learns how to push the limits, manipulate, play the system and get what he wants. As the child grows into his teenage years, he often makes bad choices and can run with the wrong crowd. Doormat parents mean well. They are often children of dictating parents and are trying to give their children the freedom and opportunities that they didn't get growing up.

Children and teenagers of doormat parents tend to...

- have a shaky sense of self; at times they feel confident and other times not;
- be unsure of where the appropriate boundaries lie between themselves and adult authority figures;
- lack respect for authority;
- be confused about what is age appropriate and what is not;
- act older than their age, sometimes younger;
- feel entitled;
- believe they are more mature and knowledgeable about the world than they actually are;
- feel very confident about making their own self-care decisions; however, they usually don't make the right, positive self-care decisions in their best interest;
- often offend adult authority figures by treating them more as friends and equals as opposed to authority figures.

Doormat Parents of Upper and Middle Class

As with dictating parents, doormat parents truly care about their children and want their children to succeed. They are compassionate, pleasing type people who want to be liked and validated. They are trying to win the approval and validation from their children. This is because they are very insecure. Unfortunately, they learn that their children don't really respect them. When their children become older, they tend to use their doormat parents as ATM machines and only seek out their parents when they want something.

Doormat Parents of Lower Class and Poverty

Very seldom will doormat parenting be found among these populations. Doormat parents care about their child's welfare. Sometimes in poor rural families, doormat parents can be found, but in larger cities, caring parents feel they need to be dictators in order to keep their children safe.

The Psyche of the Doormat Parent

Because doormat parents don't want to be dictators, like their parents were, they take parenting to the other extreme. Doormat parents also hate conflict and will easily take the blame for others mistakes and rescue others. They become lovable doormats and everyone, especially their children, walk all over them. Doormat parents do have feelings; actually they are hypersensitive. However, after being taken advantage of and walked all over for a while, the volcano erupts and they become (*for a day at most*) dictating parents, yell their heads off and become very strict. However, this doesn't do any good; their children and teenagers have learned to ignore it because they know that by tomorrow Mom and/or Dad will be apologizing profusely. The dust will settle and the doormat will be dusted off and freshly laid out to be trampled all over again. The cycle continues.

Doormat Leadership Style

The doormat leader quickly becomes a lovable doormat. They do not know how to set appropriate limits and boundaries. Doormats tend to give too much freedom because they don't want to upset people; this leads to over-indulgence and their followers quickly begin to take advantage of the situation. Followers of doormat leaders quickly learn how to manipulate their leaders and have things their way; this may not even be at a conscious level. Such leaders often act more like friends and buddies to their followers, as opposed to being an authority figure. As a result, often times the followers of doormat leaders make inappropriate choices and decisions that are not in their best interest or the best interest of the organization.

Followers of doormat leaders usually...

- tend to have a shaky sense of confidence in themselves.
- tend to make their own rules and set their own boundaries and limits, which are usually not in their best interests;
- feel entitled;
- don't always know how to make appropriate decisions;
- have a tendency to take advantage of the system.

What is the inner psyche of the doormat leader?

Doormat leaders are guilt ridden and insecure. They didn't get appropriate validation growing up, so they are looking for such volition from their followers. It is very important for them to be liked and popular by their followers. They hate conflict and avoid confrontation at all costs. They have a tendency to take the blame for others' mistakes and are always rescuing people. Hence, they become lovable doormats. After being walked all over for a time, the volcano erupts and they become tyrants and scream their heads off at everyone. They then become dictating leaders for a while and this totally confuses everyone because it is a mixed message. After which, the doormat leader calms down and feels extremely guilty. Doormat leaders are very guilt ridden.

Ghost Parenting Style....Where's Mom and Dad?

Ghosts parents are neglectful emotionally and physically. They are not involved in the lives of their children because they are too involved in their own matters. Like the other parenting styles, ghost parents come in all different shapes and sizes. They can be CEO's of major companies, alcohol and drug abusers, single parents working long and late hours or people in poverty. Ghost parents are always products of serious transgenerational attachment issues; hence, they cannot attach and be available for their own children. Children of ghost parents end up raising themselves. As a result, the child ends up confused, lost, abandoned and in trouble in one way or another. Children of ghost parents also have a tendency to become parentified children to their younger siblings. They put themselves into this role because they realize that there are no parents around and someone needs to be the parent. Sometimes parentified children of ghost parents become the parent figure to their parents, such as helping mom take a cold shower because she is "hung over" from drinking alcohol.

Children and teenagers of ghost parents tend to...

- be abandoned, neglected, abused and totally hurt;
- become parentified children;
- end up taking care of their parents, in some cases;
- have low – self esteem;
- raise themselves, which no child is capable of doing.

What is a parentified child?

A parentified child is a child who takes on the role of the parent. The child, as young as six or seven, has the responsibility of changing his baby sister's diaper and feeding the baby. The child could be a 14-year old who comes home from school and has to baby sit younger siblings, help them with their home work, feed them, bath them, etc. As a result, the child is being cheated out of his childhood. In some cases the child is taking care of his parents because they are strung out on drugs and /or alcohol, or even because they are just too lazy to take care of themselves.

Ghosts Parents of Upper and Middle Class

Ghost parents from upper and middle class are busy with their careers and social life. They often leave their children in the care of maids or relatives, while they travel the world. Sometimes drug and/or alcohol use is a factor. They provide their children with all of the material goods in the world, but they are not emotionally, and sometimes physically, not available for their children.

Ghost Parents of Lower Class and Poverty

Ghost parents from poverty are not available for their children. They are busy working jobs at odd hours. Usually, they have several children to care for. Some are on drugs and alcohol. Some are busy dating many other people. Ghost parents are often the children of ghost parents; again, it is transgenerational.

The Psyche of the Ghost Parent

Simply put, ghost parents do not know how to parent because they never experienced being parented themselves. They were left to raise themselves; hence, they leave their children to raise themselves. Ghost parents are usually hurt adults with many unresolved issues.

Ghost leaders, like ghost parents, are not around to lead. They...

- tend to pass on the leadership to their subordinates;
- tend to be busy with their own lives and work projects;

- perhaps are out of their element when leading within the given situation; hence, they have no idea how to lead.

Followers of ghost leaders usually...

- do the best that they can leading themselves;
- leave the leader by leaving the department or the company;
- find other leaders and role models either within the system or elsewhere.

What is the inner psyche of the ghost leader?

Ghost leaders do not enjoy being leaders; hence they avoid leading. On the other hand, they might also just be too involved with their own projects to worry about the people whom they are supposed to be leading.

Dictating Ghost Parent - See me this evening on SKYPE at 7:03 PM sharp

Dictating ghost parents are usually upper middle to upper class. They do everything the same way as dictating parents; however, they do so from a distance. Dictating ghosts are not physically present. Sometimes they are flying all over the world with their jobs. Other times, they are at home, but the child is away at boarding school. Dictating ghost parents are always calling, texting and SKYPING their children; they are following up on what they do at school and who their friends are. Like the dictating parent, they run the child's life.

Children and teenagers of dictating ghosts tend to...

- be abandoned and neglected;
- be wealthy (*usually*) and get satisfaction from owning material goods;
- be perfectionists;
- be insecure;
- be overachievers because they are trying to please Mom and Dad;
- become (*sometimes*) very rebellious in their teen years;
- be left to raise themselves; hence, they do not always make appropriate choices.

Dictating Ghost Parents of Upper and Middle Class

Are the same as with ghost parents.

Dictating Ghost Parents of Lower Class and Poverty

Are very rarely found in lower class and poverty.

Dictating ghost leaders, like dictating ghost parents, lead from a distance.

The dictating ghost leader is just like the dictating leader; however, he dictates via electronic devices, such as e-mails, text messaging and telephone conversations. As with the dictating leader the followers of dictating ghosts often get rebellious.

Followers of Dictating Ghost Leaders

Followers of dictating ghost leaders have the same reactions as the followers of dictating leaders. However, the follower of the dictating ghost is usually less stressed because the dictating ghost leader is not hovering around as is the dictating leader.

What is the inner psyche of the dictating ghost parent or leader?

The inner psyche of the dictating ghost is like that of the dictating parent and leader. Although, sometimes the dictating parent enjoys (*or thinks he enjoys*) parenting. The dictating ghost parent, usually, doesn't enjoy parenting but will never admit it.

The Bonded Parenting Style…. Let's talk about it.

The bonded parenting style is the preferred parenting style. Bonded parents consider parenting to be their first priority in life. They are willing to put their own needs, jobs and hobbies on hold for the sake of their children. Bonded parents place a high level of importance on listening to their children and understanding their child as a unique individual. There is never any expectation for the child to live out his parent's dreams. They do not make up personal fables about their children. Bonded parents allow freedom within age appropriate limits. This allows the child to explore and discover his talents, interests and proclivities. Bonded parents are always and forever advocates for their children in a positive way. The child is expected to own his own behavior, and the parent never rescues his child. Bonded parents are well aware that people learn best through their own mistakes. Children of bonded parents have the highest potential for reaching Marcia's identity achievement by the time they graduate from high school. Sounds impossible… not really, such parents exist. There was a TV series from 1996 – 2004, **Seventh Heaven**; this is a perfect portrayal of bonded parents. I know, the show is Hollywood; however, such families do exist.

Children and teenagers of the bonded parent tend to…

- have high self-esteem;
- feel comfortable making age appropriate decisions;
- be less rebellious;
- feel comfortable exploring new challenges;
- learn by their mistakes;
- have a realistic, true sense of self;
- enjoy teamwork;
- be less vulnerable to negative peer pressure.

Middle and Upper Class Bonded parents

Bonded parents from middle and upper class have high self-esteem. Although they have monetary means, they do not over indulge their children. They also believe that it is important for the child to learn the value of money.

Lower class and Poverty Bonded parents

Bonded parents from lower class and poverty have high self-esteem. They may not have monetary means; however, they realize that creating a home based on love and belonging cannot be bought with any amount of money; it is free. This population of bonded parents realizes the importance of braking the cycle of generational poverty (*or low socio-economic status*). They truly want their children to rise to stable middle class. They do not use their children to help support the family monetarily or by having older siblings become parentified children who raise their younger siblings.

The Psyche of the Bonded Parent

Bonded parents are happy people with high self-esteem and a strong sense of self-efficacy. They spend a lot of time honestly self-reflecting and are aware of their strengths and limitations, which they use to serve the best interest of themselves and others. Bonded parents are also aware that self-growth and realize that learning is a life long process; furthermore, they embrace the process. They also encourage the same in others.

Bonded Leadership Style

Bonded leaders are fair and impartial to the people they lead. They are aware of the different strengths and limitations among the people they lead and use this to the best interest of everyone.

Followers of bonded leaders usually…

- feel supported and confident;
- feel they can ask for help when needed;
- are clear about boundaries and limits and abide by them;
- feel they know their strengths and limitations.

What is the inner psyche of the bonded leader?

Like bonded parents, bonded leaders are happy people with high self-esteem and a strong sense of self-efficacy. They spend a lot of time honestly self-reflecting and are aware of their strengths and limitations, which they use to serve the best interest of themselves and others. Bonded leaders realize that there are different types of personality styles, working styles and learning styles; therefore, they go the extra mile to learn about these different styles in order to understand the different types of people under their leadership. Bonded leaders (*like bonded parents*) are also aware that self-growth and learning is a life long process, and they embrace the process. They also encourage the same in others.

The worst thing that any parent or leader can do is change styles from day-to-day or week-to-week. This is really confusing to the child or the person being led because the child or person being led never knows what to expect.

How would each of the above parents respond to the following situations?

Discussions on page 197 - no peeping.

1. A mother finds a test hidden in the dresser draw of her 14-year-old daughter; the child failed the test.
2. A mother of a 16-year-old boy notices marihuana in his backpack.
3. A 13-year-old-girl tells her mother that she wants to go with a 16-year-old boy to a school dance. He asked her the day before the dance.
4. A 16-year-old boy comes home smelling like cigarette smoke.
5. A 16-year-old boy decides that he wants to drop out of high school and go to automobile mechanics school.
6. An 18-year-old girl (*who still lives at home*) decides to drop out of college for at least a year so that she can find herself.
7. A 17-year-old boy wants to invest in a plant growing business with his friend. This investment will cost more than half of his college savings fund.
8. A 15-year-old girl wants to get a permanent butterfly tattoo on her right ankle.
9. You notice cuts on your 16-year-old girl's upper arm.
10. Your 15-year-old son tells you that he is spending the night with his friend. When you call the friend's house to tell your son that you will be going to the grocery store and asks what he wants for his school lunches, the friend tells you that your son is not there and there never were any plans for him to sleep over. The friend honestly has no idea where your son is. When your son comes home the next morning, you say…..
11. A mother notices her 13-year-old son has drawn a gang symbol on his hand.
12. It's been the plan for years for your 18-year-old son to attend engineering school overseas. You've worked hard and saved for 20 years to make this dream come true. He informs you that he really doesn't have the heart to study engineering. He would like to study

child development at the local university and eventually specialize in special needs education.

Now you may look at the discussions on page 199.

How would you, as a bonded mentor, respond to the of each of the following situations?

1. Your 16-year-old mentee comes to his session appearing to be "hung over."
2. You are a male mentor and your 15-year-old mentee begins coming to sessions dressed in "sexy" clothes, begins sitting closer to you and wants a hug at the beginning and end of each session.
3. Your 14-year-old mentee tells you that there is a boy in her class at school who is slipping notes into her school locker asking her to have sex with him. She shows you the note.
4. Your 15-year-old mentee tells you that he has always felt like a girl in a boy's body and wants to change his gender.
5. You are suspicious that your 13-year-old mentee might be shoplifting; she has been wearing several new earrings. She says that her friend gave them to her.
6. Your 18-year-old mentee (*of the opposite gender*) tells you that he or she appreciates how well you understand him or her. Then you get an e-mail saying how much he or she loves you and wants to thank you for your help. You helped solved all of his or her problems and now he or she wants to stop the mentor/mentee relationship and begin a friendship. What if a same gender mentee wanted this friendship (*you are both heterosexual*)?
7. Your 16-year-old mentee is dating and spending a lot of time with a person of the opposite sex. You have heard rumors about this person that you don't like from one of the mentee's neighbors.
8. Your 15-year-old mentee confesses that he has been looking at pornography sights on his computer; he can't quit.

Discussions on page 200

Self - reflective Questions:

1. What type of parents were you raised by? What was this experience like for you?
2. Were there different caregivers in your life who had different types of parenting styles? What was this experience like for you?
3. If you are a parent or caregiver, what type of parenting style do you believe you practice?
4. When you think about all the various leaders you were followers of throughout your life, which leadership styles do you remember experiencing? What were your feelings about being a follower of such leaders?
5. When leading or put in charge of others, what type of leadership style do you believe you practice? Do you find that your style changes according to the type of group you are leading?
6. What can you change about yourself and/or do to be more of a bonded type parent, leader or mentor?
7. Briefly discuss (*in your own words*) how a bonded mentor would treat his mentee?

Diana's Pearl of Wisdom - Robert Gardener said, "Children learn what they live" I would like to add "...and children live what they learn."

CHAPTER NINE

Moving on Up: Out of Generational Poverty

Introducing Dr. Ruby Payne

Ruby Payne is a former, classroom teacher, principal and school superintendent who has devoted many years to researching and understanding generational poverty. She is now retired and continues to research poverty and what it takes to make a permanent move from poverty to middle class. Ruby Payne also researches the learning styles of students from poverty backgrounds. I believe that it is important to discuss poverty because although hurt teenagers can be found in all walks of life, many who seek out mentors or who will be recommended for the mentoring program will be hurt teens from poverty.

Note: Although Payne researched and wrote her books from an American point-of-view, most aspects of her theory are universal.

Recommended books by Ruby Payne, published by Aha Press, Houston, TX.

A Framework for Understanding Poverty
Bridges out of Poverty
Removing the Mask: Giftedness in Poverty
Boys Don't Cry: Adolescent Males in Generational Poverty

Before talking about poverty lets get an understanding of what exactly constitutes middle class.

So, my question to you is "How does a person know he is middle class?"

Common answers I get, which are not really on track include…

Making a certain salary every month

Not really because money is relative. If you make 2000 dollars a month and you are a single person with no one to support but yourself, you will be able to make your financial ends meet and be considered middle class. However, you will need to count your pennies. On the other hand, if you are married with a child or two to support, you will be struggling to make ends meet; probably you would not be considered middle class.

On the other hand, if you make 6000 dollars a month and spend 7000 dollars a month, you are in debt. If you are in debt, you wouldn't be considered middle class. Especially in the modern world of plastic money (*commonly known as credit cards*) people have a tendency to begin living beyond their means. Also people in poverty have money, usually cash in large amounts. Many of them make money from working odd jobs "under the table," meaning jobs paid in cash without paying taxes. They also have material goods. I can remember working as a consultant school psychologist in a public school where the students were of low socio-economic status. Being a low-income school, 98% of the children qualified for the free lunch program and many for the free breakfast program. I remember standing in the lunch line and noticing that all the girls on free lunch were wearing more gold jewelry (*real gold - I can tell the difference*) than an Eastern Indian bride. I couldn't help but to think that if they sold their jewelry, they could buy their own lunches. Wow, all that tax money spent on free lunches surely could be put to other much needed causes. The welfare system (*at least in America*) is a system of "handouts." Handouts bread entitlement. This is where our mentees are headed unless we help them find another path; a path where they contribute to society and not look to society to "keep them."

Having a car and house to live in

Not really, people in poverty have housing and cars. Sometimes, they even have luxury cars. I can remember as a young child driving by the low-cost housing areas (*meaning government subsidized housing*) and my father would count the Cadillacs. My middle class family couldn't afford a Cadillac. My parents would often wonder how many months of rent they could have paid instead of buying a Cadillac. In short, poverty does not mean not having cash on hand.

So, what constitutes middle class?

According to Diana, a person can be considered middle class if he has the means to sustain himself and his dependents without having to rely on government funds or charity of any sort. Based on clinical observation, middle class people (*for the most part*) also have certain priorities in life. Again, I am speaking in general terms. Middle class people have a desire to better themselves in terms of knowledge and position in their careers and community. Middle class people are not content to reach a plateau and stay there. They want their children to have a better lifestyle and be more successful than they are. They also want their children to attain success and a better life through hard work and efforts. Middle class parents (*especially bonded parents*) are there for their children every step of the way and serve as moral support. Generally speaking, middle class parents don't depend on their children to help sustain them or their siblings.

Situational Poverty vs. Generational Poverty

There are two different types of poverty, situational and generational.

Situational Poverty

Situational poverty happens when a person or family is in poverty due to a unique situation that happens or an "off-scheduled" event. Such an event would be if a person falls seriously ill and can no longer work, a person's house burns down, a person looses his job or a divorce. Another example would be when a middle class person spends more than he makes or adapts a lifestyle beyond his means and as a result, the person goes bankrupt or in serious debt. Furthermore, situational poverty is for a relatively short period of time, less than two years, until the person or family can regroup and get their finances back on track. It is also important to remember that if situational poverty continues for a long period of time, it can become generational poverty.

Generational Poverty

Generational poverty, on the other hand, is inherited poverty. It is passed down from one generation to another until someone breaks the cycle. This is far easier said than done. Breaking the cycle of generational poverty requires one to change his lifestyle by closely examining his lifestyle choices and options.

According to Payne's theory, in order to make a permanent move from generational poverty to middle class, one must have two key ingredients and six personal resources.

The two key ingredients and six personal resources are...

First – Let's think – What keeps a person in poverty?

I'll give you a hint... it isn't money. People in poverty often have cash on hand. They just don't know what to do with the cash. They buy name brand clothes, fancy cars and jewelry; however, they tend not to use money on education, housing, investments, etc. Hence, what keeps a person in poverty has a lot to do with his outlook on life and his priorities, not on cash.

The **Two Key Ingredients** one must have in order to make a **PERMANENT MOVE** from poverty to middle class are...

1 – A Goal and a Plan

One must have a goal and a plan on how to attain the goal. A goal alone isn't enough. One must have a plan (*a clear understanding*) of what to do to achieve the goal. It is easy for someone to say that he wants to go to university and major in accounting. He can even be very motivated and have a clear vision of himself sitting at a desk, behind a computer, in a beautiful accounting firm working away on someone's tax returns. Yes, the dream and the vision is a very important first step in making the dream come true. Next comes the realization of the work needed to make the dream come true.

The person with this goal must next come up with a well thought out plan to achieve the goal, such as successfully completing secondary school, finding out what the entrance requirements are for the university, sourcing out scholarships, sponsorships, financial aid, etc. Then....the person must do the work to get accepted into the university and get all financial resources in order. Once he begins university, he will have to study and perhaps work part-time to help sustain himself during his university career. In short, it is a lot of work.

2 – A Significant Other

This is a person who is more than just a role model. The significant person has an up-close and personal relationship with the teen for a long time. The significant other is the wind beneath the teen's wings. He is there to pick up the teen when the "going gets tough." People in poverty experience set backs and are easily discouraged.

The significant other also serves to help the teen get in touch with his talents, interests and proclivities, find needed resources and helps him find like-minded people who will serve to help him better himself.

Speaking of which, Ruby Payne also explains that a person wanting to make a permanent move out of poverty must be willing to sever ties, either temporarily or permanently.

Payne, R. (2005). *A Framework for Understanding Poverty,* **Aha Press, Houston, TX.**

I reference to severing ties, **Diana** likes to say... the person has to be willing to change his playground and your playmates. Changing one's playground and playmates is necessary because people in poverty keep each other in poverty. Parents often encourage their teen to go to work after high school (*often times while in high school*). Why spend money on education, which costs money, then you have to wait until you finish the education in order to begin making money? This requires delayed gratification. Please remember, people in poverty have a difficult time with delayed gratification. Also, this allows for the working teen to help with the household finances. The teen can go to work and make enough money in a month to pay the rent and the electric bill.

The teen's peers will also encourage him to "stay in the neighborhood." People in poverty are more tribal. They feel very betrayed when someone wants to better himself and leave the neighborhood. At times, there might be aspects of envy because someone has an opportunity to better himself; however, usually it is about "leaving the group." There is a sense of extended family among people in poverty and when one leaves the neighborhood, the people of the neighborhood feel abandoned and betrayed

In the 2001 movie, ***Save the Last Dance*** (*this movie will be further discussed in Chapter 12*) a white, adolescent girl has to suddenly move to an inner-city neighborhood and live with her estranged father after her mother dies in a car crash. This is one of those "off-scheduled" events that placed Sarah in a state of situational poverty. She does an excellent job of maintaining her healthy, true sense of self and not being persuaded by the unsavory environment around her. As the story continues, she develops a close friendship with an African American boy named Derrick; they both share a love for dance. Derrick, aspires to be a medical doctor and receives a scholarship from Georgetown University. Derrick, who is being raised by his grandmother, has a strong support system in his grandmother. She is very supportive of Derrick's desire to break the cycle of generational poverty. However, many of Derrick's friends try to persuade him to stay in the neighborhood by saying that college is for white folks and that he won't be accepted there.

Six Personal Resources

Ruby Payne further explains that a person wishing to make a permanent move out of generational poverty must also have the following six personal resources.

1 – Financial: This means the funds a person needs to fund his post-secondary education or job training courses, as well as, the funds to sustain himself while pursuing his goals. This does not only mean cash money. Financial resources include scholarships, sponsorships, or low - interest government educational loans.

2 – Educational: This begins with basic education and the knowledge of reading and writing. A person has to know how to read and write in order to fill out the job application, even for a minimum wage job. Then of course there remains a high coloration between higher levels of education and earning potential. Therefore, the more education one has - the more marketable he is and the more earning potential he has.

As we all know hurt teens can be very rebellious about education. They don't want to go to school, and they certainly don't want to hear about school. Like anything else, lecturing them about the importance of getting a good education usually falls on deaf ears. As the teen becomes more secure within himself through his trust in his mentor as the significant other in his life, he will be more open to hearing about the importance of education. If you are fortunate enough to have a mentee with supportive parents or guardians, then you will also be able to enlighten his parents or guardians about the importance of education.

It has also been my experience with several hurt teens that once the teen gets excited about learning a trade or participating in an extra-curricular activity that he likes, he will become more motivated about education. Meaning, with hurt teens, sometimes taking an interest in education can work in reverse order. Instead of education inspiring the teen to be interested in an activity, higher education or learning a trade, the opposite happens. Meaning, because the hurt teen first develops a desire to participate in an activity, go to college or learn a trade, this inspires him to take an interest in school.

3 – Physical Health: It is important to maintain good physical health through proper diet, exercise and regular health checkups. There is usually free medical care in all areas, so money shouldn't be an object. People of poverty usually don't care or want to be bothered with regular doctors visits; often time, they forget about regular routine checkups (*oops, so do I, personal confession*).

4 – Role Models: These are the people a person admires and aspires to be like. Unlike a significant other with whom someone has a close and personal relationship, a role model can be someone the person has never met. Maybe the role model is a person who has been dead for several years. Many Americans consider Abraham Lincoln to be a role model or Mother Theresa. Role models can also be international celebrities. A role model can also be a fictional character from a movie or novel. Having role models gives us a human, concrete representation of what we admire and hope to become. It is important to remember that a role model is not the same as a significant other. All significant others are role models; however, not all role models are significant others (*remember, the poodle- dog analogy*). A significant other is an up-close, one-to-one, face-to-face relationship; a role model does not have to be a face-to face relationship.

5– Emotional Health: It is important to have someone to go to for emotional support when times get tough, a support system of people who will be there, unconditionally for us during the hard times. For many of us this is our family. For people in poverty (*and also people of other socio-economic classes*) this isn't always the case, due to ghost parenting, dictating parenting, or just not being able to tune into the child or teenager (*or even other adults*).

6 – Spiritual: Having a spiritual resource is not to be confused with religious followings and practices. Although, many people define their sense of spirituality by following a certain religious practice; this is fine. However, a spiritual resource is a belief in a higher power that transcends Earth and is unconditionally loving, omnipresent and always with you. You can call upon this higher power whenever needed. For many people, the higher power is God; however, it doesn't have to be. It is also very important to have a way to connect with your higher power, either through prayer, meditation, drumming, chanting, whirling, shaking rattles under a full moon….. whatever works.

It is **VERY IMPORTANT** to remember that hurt teenagers tend to be very rebellious against spiritual and/or religious issues. They don't want to be told what God, Allah, Jesus, Jehovah, this Guru or that Guru can do for them. They always think, where was this "higher power" when mom and dad abandoned me, when my sister was killed, etc. In short, generally speaking, they **are not ready** to have faith of any kind. My recommendation is to let your mentee come around on his own time and terms. If he asks you to discuss a certain religion or spiritual concept with him, do so from his point-of- view, devoid of any judgment. Help him to explore his spiritual and religious curiosities for himself. Sometimes the teen will bring up the subject of spirituality or religion and ask questions, such as "Do you believe in God?" or "What religion are you?" My suggestion is to answer in a very generic sense such as for the question "What religion are you?" Answer, "I respect all religions." If he or she probes further, then reflect back on him by saying, "What have been your thoughts on ....."

These questions could be coming from a few different places within your mentee. Such as, he might be asking you because he is truly curious. On the other hand, this could be a means to probe into you and test you, especially if he has had negative experiences with religion or someone forcing religion on him. So, he will test you to know where you stand with religion and see if you are going to be someone who will force religion on him.

Based on clinical observation (*actually, based on life observation*), religion can't be forced on anyone, especially not a hurt teen. Please remember that just because someone is indoctrinated from birth into a certain religion (*he usually doesn't have a choice*) doesn't mean that the person has sincerely, internalized the religion. Back to religion and hurt teens... we will all do much better by serving as a spiritual role model and walking the walk as opposed to merely talking the talk. Now, I also understand that with some people there may be a very visible, telltale sign showing their religious preferences based on clothing or ornaments. Sheiks cover their hair and wear a silver bangle around their wrist, female Muslims wear hijabs, and female Hindus wear a Bindi, (*red if married or another color if single*). In such cases, your mentee will be well aware of your religious preference. This is fine; I am not suggesting that you hide yourself. However, it is important to let your mentee know that you are open-minded and will not impose any certain religion on him. In short, forcing or pushing any religion or religious beliefs on a hurt teen will only bring resentment. Please believe me on this one.

Payne, R. (2005). *A Framework for Understanding Poverty,* Aha Press, Houston, TX.

Read the following case scenarios and discuss which of the six resources the teen and his family has and which resources need to be obtained or attained.

NOTE: All case scenarios written below are fictitious.

Case of Kumar and Licha

Kumar is a 14-year- old boy. His mother and father have been divorced for 10 years. His father has remarried and pays minimal child support each month; some months he pays none. Kumar's mother, Licha, works as a cashier at a bakery and is a recovering alcoholic. Kumar has a half sister, Pryia, who is eight. She has Cerebral Palsy and is wheel chair bound. Pryia was born out of wedlock. Pryia's father ran off after Licha told him she was pregnant; he hasn't been seen or heard from since. Licha was married to Kumar's father, Rajan, for five years. Three of those years, Kumar was in law school and working internships long hours each day. Licha would have a few drinks to calm her loneliness.

Kumar was also born during that time, and Licha was often left alone to take care of him, since Rajan was out of the house so much. When Rajan finished his internship, he announced that he was in love with a fellow intern *(with whom he had been having an affair for two years)* and wanted a divorce. The last Licha heard, her ex- husband was working in a private firm, driving a BMW, living in a three-story townhouse in an up-scaled neighborhood and taking yearly vacations with his wife to Europe and Latin America.

Licha's parents are both dead; she has an older sister who lives 200 kilometers away. They haven't spoken in twelve years, since Licha started drinking. Licha's monthly income including child support is 1,200 dollars per month after taxes. Kumar attends public school. Licha attends public school for handicapped students and then goes to a baby sitter after school hours. The babysitter is a retired 65-year-old woman. The fee is eight dollars per hour. The elderly baby sitter is often sick, so Kumar is expected to take care of is sister when he comes home from school.

The family's current situation

Licha has missed five days of work this month due to illness of either herself or Pryia. Licha's boss has begun to cut her pay each time she misses or is late. Even if she brings a medical certificate, the boss said that she is sick too much.

If this keeps up, she will be fired. Licha's car engine died last week, and it is beyond repair. Therefore, transportation to work is now a problem. There is a new girl who moved into the apartment next door to Licha. Her name is Sally, and she wants to introduce Licha to her boyfriend's brother. Licha doesn't want to date anyone because as soon as the guy finds out about her two children, one of whom is handicapped, the guy will no longer be interested in her. She has given up on guys and dating. Pryia has been put on a new, alternative medicine that costs 100 dollars each month; welfare won't cover the cost because the medicine is still in the experimental stage.

Kumar comes home from school and announces that the students are going on a weekend camping trip to learn about ecology and do team building games. He really wants to go, but the total cost is 150 dollars. Kumar usually helps watch Pryia on weekends, while Licha works. Her ex has threatened to take her to court and say that she is an unfit mother if she tries to get money from him. While Licha is trying to figure out her situation, Sally calls and invites Licha to go on a double date with her; Sally's boyfriend's brother would be Licha's date. Licha hasn't dated anyone in the past six years. Licha saw the guy briefly a couple of months ago; he helped Sally move into her apartment. He is really handsome. Licha decides to go.

Think about the following.

Discuss the family resources; what resources do they have and what resources are needed?
What would be a realistic way for the family to go about obtaining/attaining the needed resources?
Discuss what makes Kumar a hurt teen.
Is it a good idea for Licha to begin dating again? Explain.
What would you recommend to Licha to help the family? Explain.

The Case of Ling Ling and Su Lin

Ling Ling is a 13-year-old girl of Chinese decent; she lives with her maternal grandmother. Su Lin is a 70-year-old widow who lives on her retirement pension of 800 dollars per month. All of her siblings have past. Ling Ling's mother was put in jail at the age of 23 when Ling Ling was 18-months old.

Ling Ling's mother, who was a victim of extreme domestic violence, hit her abusive husband over the head with a hammer while he was sleeping. This left him brain damaged and unable to speak or function as an adult. Mom is now in jail for life. Ling Ling never sees her mother. She has been told that both of her parents died in a car crash. Ling Ling has a picture of her mother holding her when Ling Ling was a baby. Ling Ling often looks at the picture at night before she goes to bed; sometimes she cries. Su Lin see's her crying but doesn't know what to say, so she pretends not to notice. Su Lin believes that within time, Ling Ling will get over her mother.

Current Situation

Su Lin has recently joined her community's Christian church. She has found an inner sense of peace in her fellowship with Jesus and also participates in the senior members social service group. Two years ago, Su Lin was hit by a slow moving car while walking across the parking lot of a grocery store; pedestrians had the right of way. Her right leg was broken. Two days ago Su Lin heard from her lawyer that her lawsuit was finally settled out of court and she will receive 18,000 dollars in damages. She can finally pay off her debts, buy some new clothes for Ling Ling and begin a college fund for Ling Ling. Su Lin's, church members have learned about her lawsuit settlement and are beginning to ask for loans. Su Lin wants to help her church members, who have always been there for her, but she really doesn't want to lend any money. She needs this money for herself and Su Lin. For now she is putting off the request by saying that the check hasn't cleared the bank. She knows that this excuse won't last for long. Her church friends have been very good to her; she would hate to loose them.

Think about the following.

Discuss the family resources. What resources do they have and what resources are needed?
What would be a realistic way for the family to go about obtaining/attaining the needed resources?
Discuss what makes Ling Ling a hurt teen.
Should Su Lin lead any money to her church friends? Explain.
What would you recommend to Su Lin to help the family? Explain.

The Case of Afiq and Norani

Afiq is a 16-year-old teenager who lives with his mother, Norani, his father (*when he is around*) and his four younger siblings. His father is often away on business; he works in import and export services. He doesn't really interact much with the family when he is home; he says that he is tired from working long hours. He shuts himself up in his bedroom and either watches TV or reads magazines. Afiq dropped out of high school to help out around the house because his Dad is gone so often. The family moved to a state far away from any extended family members because of Dad's work. The nearest extended relative is 200 miles away. No one has been able to make friends. Mom is working as a hawker selling fruit to make some extra money. Mom is a very devote Muslim and has raised her children in the faith. Norani attends the lady's Quran readings every Thursday evening at the neighborhood mosque. Sometimes Afiq's sisters go along. The sisters never really talk much about religion; it is always the mom reminding everyone about prayer time. At mom's insistence, Afiq regularly attends the Friday mid-day service at the mosque for men. If Dad is around, he will also go. Dad makes good money, but he keeps it in the bank. He says that he is keeping it for retirement. Norani does her best to support the family on the money she makes being a hawker.

Current Situation

Norani has been diagnosed with breast cancer and needs to undergo chemotherapy for the next year. Her sister has offered to come live with the family and help Norani while she is sick and undergoing treatment. Afiq now has to work and oversee the hawker stand while Mom is sick. He just enrolled in a part-time automobile mechanics certification program at night. He is hoping to work in the field. Now he has to drop the program so that he can work the hawker stand. Hopefully, he can take the course next year.

Think about the following.

Discuss the family resources. What resources do they have and what resources are needed?
What would be a realistic way for the family to go about obtaining/attaining the needed resources?

Discuss what makes Afiq a hurt teen.

Discuss the parenting styles of Afiq's mother and father.

What would you recommend to Norani to help the family situation?

The Case of Liz and Cindy

Cindy is a 17-year-old girl living in a children's shelter home. She has lived in the shelter home since she was 11. Liz, her mother, brought her to the shelter home when her father walked out on the family and went to live with his new girlfriend in another state far away. At the time, Liz was jobless and had no means to support Cindy. Her mother tries to see Cindy on holidays, but her new boyfriend is not fond of kids. This new guy is a good guy. He pays most of the bills and is faithful to Liz. Liz believes that once the relationship is more stable, she will be able to help Cindy and her new boyfriend connect. Right now Liz feels that what is most important is for her to build a good relationship with her new boyfriend because he is a really good guy.

Cindy loves to do hair and makeup. She is always practicing on the other girls in the home. She has been accepted into beauty school and there is a family willing to sponsor her schooling fees. Lately Cindy has been saying that she doesn't know for sure if this is what she wants to do.

The housemother has noticed that Cindy has been cutting herself with the end of her keychain. Cindy was working with an intern counselor from a local university for six months and making progress, but the intern completed her hours two-months ago and is no longer working with Cindy. This is when the cutting started. The home takes the children to church every Sunday. The leader of the church's youth group, Cindy's confidant, left to study overseas. One of Cindy's roommates tells the home administrator that Cindy has said she wants to kill herself.

Think about the following.

Discuss the Cindy's resources; what resources do they have and what resources are needed?

What would be a realistic way for Cindy to go about obtaining/attaining the needed resources?

Discuss the Cindy's relationship with her mother.

Discuss what makes Cindy a hurt teen.

What resources does Cindy need?

Look on page 201 and see if we agree.

Being a mentor is about becoming the significant other in your mentee's life. If you are working with a teen (*who is still living with his mother and/or father*) ideally the work is about helping the parent(s) become a significant other. This won't be possible in some cases; however, every now and then there is a case where the parents are open to guidance, and this is a very rewarding experience for all. It is a very thrilling experience when the parents, mentor and teen work together as a team. Remember, the most important task for the mentor of a hurt teen is to help the teen find his needed resources.

Self - reflective Questions:

1. What have been your experiences with generational poverty?
2. What resources did you have as a teen? How did you go about finding your needed resources?
3. If not your parents, who was the "significant other" in your life?
4. Discuss your six personal resources today. Are there any resources you need more of in some way? Yes, we all need more money, what else?

Diana's Pearls of Wisdom – To move onward and upward in life, we must be willing to change our playmates and our playground. With this comes the realization that some of our old playmates will be gone forever.

CHAPTER TEN

Maslow: Working to my Fullest Potential

Cultivating an Environment of Love and belonging vs. Mere Cattle Care

I have been in many houses of many families throughout my lifetime in many different parts of the world. Meaning, I was in these houses just as a visitor and not any type of professional "checking out" something. However, I am trained in family dynamics; hence, it is second nature for me to notice the interactions between and among the different family members. What I have often noticed is that many times each family member is off in his own space doing some solitary activity: mom is talking on the phone to her friend, dad is watching TV as he pets the family dog, little Susie is playing with Barbie dolls, and big brother Joe is playing a video game. The family members are not interacting with each other. I have also noticed that when parents are communicating with their children, it is to tell them that it is time to clean up for dinner, get busy with their homework, help Mom with the dishes and get packed for soccer practice.

It's all about directing, guiding and keeping the order just like a captain on a ship. Seldom is everyone sitting as a group, tuning into each other, discussing the day or participating in a group activity just for the fun of it. Maybe this isn't the case in your home, but it does happen in many homes of all socio-economic classes around the world. I also notice that parents don't take the time to interact with each child on a one-to-one basis. When parents are interacting with their children and teenagers one-to-one, they are (*often times*) correcting their behavior, discussing a problem at school, helping the child or teen with his homework, reminding the child or teen to finish his science project or reminding him to take out the trash. Simply put, one-to-one connection is about correcting a problem or reminding the child or teen about his responsibilities. Unfortunately, it is not so common for parents to take the time to interact and connect one-to-one with their children and teenagers in order to listen to the wonderful science experiment that won second place at the school science fair, building something out of Lego blocks together, reading a book together or polishing each other's nails. This happens because parents are **TOO BUSY.** Then the same parents wonder why their child or teenager spends so much time on the internet or playing video games. **Need I say more....**

I remember a lovely couple whose 10-year-old son, Paul (*not his real name*) was in therapy with me for rebellious behaviors at home. The family was of upper-middle class and very well educated; Paul was very intellectually gifted and talented. Furthermore, Paul had all the material toys, goods and comforts under the sun and the moon and the stars, to say the least. What he didn't have was his parent's validation, time and attention. There was also a younger sister in the family who seemed to be the "favored" child because she didn't have acting out behaviors. Hence, the more praise the sister received, the more Paul acted out; it was a catch 22 situation.

So, I explained to the parents during a parent consultation session what I perceived was the cause of Paul's behavior at home and the importance of the parents changing the way they interact with Paul. I suggested that we begin by the mother spending 15 minutes a day, four times a week engaging in an activity of Paul's choosing. The only guidelines were that the activity couldn't consist of any teaching, learning or guiding from Mom; however, it is alright if Paul teaches his mother something. Also, Mom had to give 100 percent full attention to Paul and the activity. The mother first responded by saying, "It is just so hard to find the time." I responded, diplomatically, "Children take time." Mom then nodded in agreement; she "got it." What crossed my mind at the time was that I really couldn't believe my ears. Here was an intelligent, high functioning mother who was afraid that she couldn't find a total of one hour a week to spend time with her son. She was a stay at home mom. I mean... honestly...I really had trouble with this one. As the story continues, Mom did begin to spend time with Paul at his level and so did Dad. Progress was made over the next year; Paul's oppositional behaviors improved. Then the family moved to another country. Paul continued to work well with the school counselor in his new school.

I would also like to share another true story about Mary (*not her real name*) who was raising three children between the ages of six to thirteen. Mary was in therapy with me because after fourteen years of marriage, her husband decided to divorce her so that he would be free to date his new office assistant. Her ex-husband was very stingy with the finances, so Mary had to work two jobs to support herself and her three children. Working a total of 50 hours a week between the two jobs was not only making Mary stressed, but it did not leave Mary any time with her children. Mary decided to quit one of her jobs and move in with her sister, who was also a single parent with one child. Together both ladies co-parented the four children and pooled their finances to pay the bills. This left both ladies more time with their children. In short, where there is a will, there is a way...**BE CREATIVE.**

What cultivates a sense of love and belonging for all children and teenagers is consistent one-to- one connection over the first 18 years of the child's life. Please continue even after the first eighteen years, as much as possible. This is an innate need that all human beings have and never outgrow, meaning this one-to-one exclusive connection. For without this one-to-one connection, parents and caregivers are merely providing cattle care for their children and teenagers.

What is cattle care?

A cattle is a herd of cows that are cared for by merely being kept. They are fed and housed (*very well I must say*) until they are fat enough to be sent to the butcher's house. Of course we don't send humans to butchers; however, if all we do as parents is give them shelter (*even in large mansions)* feed them, cloth them, send them to school and even buy them all the latest gadgets and material items without the quality one-to-one connection, we are treated them as cattle. This might not happen in your home, but it does happen in many homes. As with the story of Paul, his oppositional behavior was his outcry against being raised in cattle care fashion, devoid of emotional love and belonging. Of course his parents did love him, but they didn't understand how Paul needed to be loved....GI^2.

Please remember that no amount of money in the world can buy love and belonging. Love and belonging is priceless. We can go into the poorest, indigenous villages where people do not have a penny to spare and find children and teenagers who have secure attachments and a sense of love and belonging. On the other hand, we can go to the mansions of Malibu Beach where people are multi-millionaires and find many hurt children and teenagers being raised in cattle care fashion. Hurt teenagers are products of cattle care upbringing; hence, it is the duty of we mentors to provide a sense of love and belonging with the teen through consistent, on going one- to-one connection over a loooooooooooooong period of time.

In short, we must all go beyond cattle care when helping a hurt teen. Cattle care nurturance (*which isn't nurturance*) will never create a feeling of love and belonging within any teen. May I say again to all mentors of hurt teens, the teens we mentor are hurt because they have been raised in cattle care fashion; many haven't even been feed and clothed properly. Therefore, our main objective is to make that one-to-one connection so that your mentee can begin to feel a sense of love and belonging.

The next important step in our work is to help the hurt teen find the appropriate support groups, such as sports teams, teen leadership programs, extra-curricular activities, etc. in order to give them group support. Teens will find a group to identify with. If it isn't a productive group, they will surely find a non-productive group, such as a street gang. That is what gangs do for the hurt teen, the gang (*his bros*) gives him a sense of love and belonging. What a terrible place to cultivate a sense of love and belonging. Often times, in such situations, the next group he belongs to is his cellmates in the penitentiary.

Abraham Maslow – American Psychologist

Abraham Maslow's (1908 – 1970) is another "oldie but goodie;" however, he is also ageless and timeless. He is best known for his theory of self-actualization. His theory is based on the assumption that it is the innate drive for each human being to aspire to be highly self-aware and achieve his best. In short, to always reach beyond his grasp. However, in order to be operating at his full potential, a person must be free from having to spend his emotional energy on meeting his physical and survival needs. These are his basic needs. Then he must also have a strong sense of self and high self-esteem; healthy, high self- esteem I must add. Gang members have high self-esteem; however, it is unhealthy, high self-esteem (*a product of the false self*). Healthy self- esteem is an outgrowth of having a secure sense of love and belonging. It is then that he has the strength and energy to stand straight and tall, with his head held high so he can reach beyond his grasp and be on a journey of self -actualization.

Below is the hierarchy of Maslow's Self- Actualization Theory.

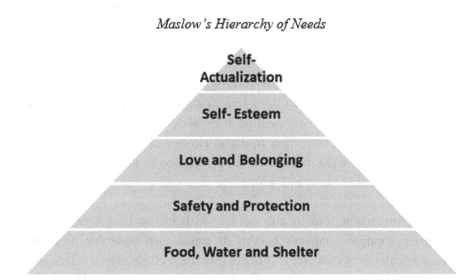

Maslow's Hierarchy of Needs

Maslow, A. (1954). *Motivation and Personality,* **Harper Publishers, New York, NY.**

Question – At what point do humans surpass animals in the wild?

The answer is **love and belonging.** Now, I must remind you that I am talking about animals in the wild. I do not mean domesticated house pets, like your cute little puppy, Fifi, or your adorable furry cat, Elmo. Several of my friends have such pets who have more love and belonging than many humans do. When I was a teenager and young adult, my parents had an adorable, white toy poodle, Monique. Monique would lick off my father's ice-cream cone with my father's full consent. Dad never let me lick off his ice-cream cone, seriously.

These pets are very fortunate with great karma, and I couldn't be happier for them. Sorry, I am off topic.

Back to animals in the wild…animals in the wild have the first two levels of Marlow's hierarchy met. They know how to find food, water and shelter, and they also know how to keep themselves safe from environmental elements and predators. However, there is no love and belonging beyond a very short time after birth. Wild animals quickly leave their mothers after birth; once they do, they don't look to return to their mothers. Mating is strictly biological for procreation. When they do instinctual come together in herds or packs or dens, it is for protection and survival. Daily live is about day-to-day survival for animals in the wild.

Hurt teens are often in survival mode; hence, they have manipulating and controlling behaviors. Like animals in the wild, they live in survival mode. It is their internal struggle of trying to get their emotional needs met (*and sometimes physical needs*) that causes the acting out behaviors. I must also add that the teen, usually, doesn't even realize that he is acting out. Acting out has become a second nature survival tool.

So, what hope is there for the teenager who has been raised in a cattle care fashion and is thus a hurt teen? How do we cultivate an environment of love and belonging for a teen?

The good news is that in many cases there is hope; it isn't too late providing the teen is motived and is not involved in drugs, crime and/or truancy from school. If the teen has been involved in such unsavory behaviors, as long as it's in the past and he is now willing to forever change his playground and his playmates, there is still hope. He needs a secure base attachment (*a significant other adult*) to whom he can go to in times of need and be 100% convinced that he will be unconditionally heard, understood, guided, loved, and not be "given up on" 100% of the time (*24-7-365 including public holidays*). This is the doorway for building his self-esteem.

Moving up the hierarchy - What is self-esteem?

The *English Collin Dictionary* (2014) defines self-esteem "Respect for or a favorable opinion of oneself. Confidence, faith in one's self, self-assurance."

I think of self-esteem in terms of high self- efficacy, having the belief in yourself that you can be successful and are a worthy person. You know that you are not perfect, but you are aware of your limitations and have realistic (*yet challenging*) expectations for yourself.

What builds self-esteem in hurt teenagers?

First the teen must have a sense of love and belonging. If we try to enhance a hurt teen's self- esteem before he has a true sense of love and belonging, we will once again be putting the cart before the horse. Also, the teen needs a significant adult (*like a mentor*) to whom he can turn when times are tough. The mentor serves as a cheerleader who cheers him on. The mentor understands where the teen has been and where it is best for him to go. The mentor accepts the unique individual the teen has become and still invites him to grow through his true talents, interests and proclivities. It is also important to remember that self-esteem develops over one's entire lifespan.

It is also important to remember that a key component in building self-esteem is having a sense of autonomy. A teenager who lives in an environment where he is always being dictated to, told what to do and have all decisions made for him is at risk for having low self-esteem. The teenager might feel a sense of love and belonging; however, being given age appropriate choses is what builds healthy self-esteem. Again, I must remind everyone that dictating parents have the best of intentions; they are just...well...GI[2]. Having a sense of autonomy allows us to reflect upon our past success and use these successful experiences as the foundation from which to build more successful experiences. Likewise, having a sense of autonomy allows us to reflect upon our mistakes and use these experiences as growth and learning experiences as well.

Moving on to the next stage in Maslow's hierarchy, self actualization...

Having a healthy, high self-esteem serves as the foundation from which a person launches his journey of self-actualization.

What is self-actualization?

It may be loosely described as the full use and exploitation of one's talents, interests and proclivities. Maslow defines self-actualization as follows, "… capabilities and potentialities. Such people seem to be fulfilling themselves and to be doing the best that they are capable of doing. They are people who have developed or are developing to the full stature of which they are capable."

Maslow, A. (1954). *Motivation and Personality,* **Harper Publishers, New York, NY.**

I like to think of self-actualization as a life long journey. It is that path that we are traveling when we are functioning at our best. We never finish evolving or achieving throughout our lives. As soon as we achieve one goal as we travel down our self-actualizing path, we set a new goal. The journey never Ends… "until death do us part." Maybe it even continues after death…?

Being on a self-actualizing path also involves becoming aware of our true self. We become who we are, understand what our strengths and limitations are and begin to put these to work in our best interests. As with Maslow's hierarchy, we must first have a strong sense of self-esteem to be on our journey of self-actualization and even realize what our self-actualizing journey means for us. However, I must say again, self-esteem is an outgrowth of love and belonging. To build self-esteem, we must feel safe and know that if a mistake is made or if something does not go well, we have a support system readily available at all times.

For healthy teenagers growing up in healthy, supportive environments, love and belonging, self-esteem and self-actualization are all cogs on the same wheel; however, the foundation is always love and belonging. For hurt teenagers, a foundation of love and belonging must first be laid before they can begin to build a sense of healthy, high self-esteem and be on a self-actualizing path.

Self – reflection Questions:

1. Discuss your journey of self-actualization.
2. When you were a teenager, where did you find love and belonging?

3. Did you believe that as a teenager you were on a self-actualizing path?
4. How do you believe you will be able to contribute to your mentee beginning to feel a sense of love and belonging, enhancing his self-esteem and help him begin his journey of self-actualization?

Diana's Pearls of Wisdom - Having a sense of love and belonging is the foundation from which we develop healthy, high self-esteem, which then propels our journey of self-actualization.

CHAPTER ELEVEN

Sexual Identity, Sexual Preference and the Dating Scene

It's universal, by the age of 14 (*give or take a year*) teenagers have been through puberty; meaning, the pituitary gland has engaged. The teen now has the urge to be physically intimate; this is universal and eternal. The cave men (*and cave women, too*) experienced feelings of arousal, man (*and women, too*) experience it today and if there is a world 2000 years from now (*you'll be dead, and I'll be busy writing another book*), men and women will have feelings of arousal. OK, enough biology; I am quickly getting out of my league. I apologize to the science community for my layman's vernacular. Simply put, people are sexual beings (*so are animals, but I will stick to discussing humans*) and we all have feelings of arousal.

Teenagers today *(and even young children)* are very exposed to sex, including the good, the bad, the pretty and the ugly. Hence, what is good, bad, right or wrong can be very confusing to them. We also realize that what is right or wrong is subjective depending upon personal values, cultural and religious/ spiritual beliefs. What we, as adults, also have to remember is that our feelings and beliefs about sexual morality are not necessarily going to be the beliefs and feelings of the teenagers for whom we care and mentor.

Sex is a very powerful drive in all human beings. It becomes even more powerful when it comes to hurt teens. Hurt teens have lived a life whereby they feel very unloved and unwanted. Generally speaking, they are hungry for love and belonging...remember that third level of Maslow's hierarchy of needs? Hence, they are vulnerable to sexual relationships, which are not positive ones.

We as adults know that sex does not equate to love and being genuinely cared for. However, to the unloved teen, a sexual encounter can be a powerful source of validation, appreciation and feeling a sense of love and belonging. To the hurt teen (*who not only has raging hormones but also feels unloved*) this can be total ecstasy.

So, what is the mentor's role in the sex life his mentee?

Nothing, unless it becomes an issue in some way, and 9.99999999 times out of 10 the issue of sex will come up (*either directly or indirectly*). This will especially be the case if you have developed trust and rapport with your mentee.

Issues that are likely to arise are usually...

- self-disclosure about their sexual experiences, which might not be totally true – remember the personal fable;
- asking you questions about your sex life and sexual experiences (*don't disclose*);
- asking for advice on whether or not it is OK to engage in sex with his or her boyfriend or girlfriend;
- asking what they should do because they are being sexually harassed;
- asking about birth control and sexually transmitted diseases;
- disclosure of past and/or present sexual abuse;
- confusion about his sexual orientation;
- confusion about his gender.

For those of you who are mentoring through a particular religious organization and part of your mission is religious guidance (*within the practices of that faith*) then go with that. I am also assuming that your mentee has chosen this religious path of his own free will and wishes to be guided accordingly. If not, you will just be another "irritating adult" trying to run his life, and he will rebel. On the other hand, if you are both on the same page in terms of spiritual beliefs and the morals and values that go hand-in-hand with those beliefs.... go for it. But please, do not think that this will stop a hungry teen (*who is looking for love, belonging and validation*) from eventually engaging in sexual activity. Have you ever seen a thirsty horse drink water?

For those of you not mentoring through any religious organization, I suggest that you remain value neutral on the moral issues of sex. If the teen has a certain religious/spiritual path that he is committed to, help him follow the morals associated with sexual activity based on that faith, whether you believe in it or not. It is about the teen, and **NEVER** about you in any way, shape or form...**FULL STOP.**

But **PLEASE** religious beliefs or no religious beliefs, do not begin and end with what I call the "cop out" answer, which is sex is only the "right thing" to do if you are married. Then end the conversation there. This is a perfectly fine moral belief; however, just because two people are married doesn't necessarily make the sexual union between the two of them safe and non-abusive.

What am I talking about ...

From where I stand, a sexual union is safe and non-abusive when two consenting adults agree to the union, understand all possible consequences of the union (*both good and bad*) and are willing to accept responsibility for any consequences that occur as a result of this union (*good or bad*). Furthermore, the two consenting adults have discussed a plan (*upon which they both agree*) as to what to do about any consequences should they occur. Now, if on top of all of the aforementioned the consenting adults are married...this is all the better. However, just because the two consenting adults are married, it doesn't mean that the above aforementioned is automatically in place; sometimes it is not.

In many marriages, the husband and wife (*assuming it is a heterosexual marriage*) are not on the same page in terms of their sexual practices. One person forces unwanted sexual styles on the other and/or forces birth control or the lack of birth control on the other, etc. I consider both of these to be examples of sexual abuse, even though the couple is in a legal marriage contract. I'll discuss more about sex abuse in a few pages. Again, as for the moral issues of right and wrong, stay neutral on this one. It is OK to discuss the risk factors with your mentee, such as....

- unwanted pregnancy;
- sexually transmitted diseases;

- feelings of feeling used, abandoned, abused, etc;
- help in seeking the appropriate resources for birth control.

Discussing sex with teenagers

If the teen discloses that he is sexually active, don't be judgmental; please be sure that she (*if you are mentoring a female*) is seeing a gynecologist. If your mentee is breaking the law via prostitution, you have a duty to warn. Please report to the appropriate authority. Your job is to build up the teen's self esteem so that they don't need to get validated in such an "un-validating" way.

From my first book – ***Understanding and Caring for the Hurt Child***

Discussing sex with teenagers

10 – 13 years – Their hormones are raging at this time.

Ages 10 -13 is the typical age range when children become sexually curious. If they ask you questions, answer them honestly an appropriately.

At this age it is important for the pre-teen to begin…

- learning about the body changes experienced during puberty, and what this is all about;
- learning about sex and sexuality, pregnancy and transmitted sexual diseases/infections; talk openly and frankly with the child about what sexual intimacy is and what it is not;
- to be prepared for and understand menstruation (*for girls*) and nocturnal ejaculation (*for boys*).

How do we do this?

I recommend buying age appropriate books that explain this in a realistic and honest manner. It is best to read the book with the young teen. Sexual orientation will also begin to emerge at this time. If the subject comes up, speak honestly and frankly. Do not judge regardless of your thoughts on "atypical" sexual orientations.

14 – 18 years – They are usually through puberty at this time.

Let us not be naïve and think that just because we tell teenagers not to have sex, they are not going to engage in sexual activity. It is better to give them the whole picture and encourage them to make intelligent choices. They will make their own choice whether right, wrong, good bad or indifferent. What is most important is that mentors give their mentees accurate information.

At this age, teenagers…

- should know the different methods of birth control;
- should have knowledge of sexually transmitted diseases;
- should start seeing an obstetrician and gynecologist (OBGYN) if a female;
- should be encouraged to have appropriate platonic interactions with the opposite sex or same sex if this is his orientation;
- should be made aware of how they will be tempted by peers and/ or the media. The forbidden can be very tempting.

Help your mentee understand that his sexual orientation is emerging and that not everyone is straight. Even when girls are alone with girls and boys are alone with boys, sexual pressures can be an issue.

Baranovich, D. (2013), *Understanding and Caring for the Hurt Child,* **Pearson Publishing, Singapore.**

Sex Abuse – Unfortunately, many hurt teens have been victims of sex abuse to some extent. In short, this really causes a lot of issues in regard to their feelings about physical intimacy. If the abuse is something that is happening in the present, you have a duty to warn. You, as the mentor, must report to the appropriate authorities for further investigation. This can be difficult when the perpetrator is someone your mentee cares about and doesn't want to see get into any sort of trouble. However, part of being a mentor is helping to empower your mentee to take care of himself. Also your mentee might be afraid of what the perpetrator will do to him if "the secret" gets out. When reporting, make sure that the teen is protected. How this is accomplished depends upon which country and where within the country you and your mentee are living. Please do your homework about "the system" and the reliability of "the system."

If the abuse was something that happened in the past and your mentee is no longer at risk of being violated (*at least not by this particular perpetrator*) just be there to listen. In either of the above cases, it is recommended that your mentee receive professional therapy from a qualified professional who has experience working with victims of sex abuse. The other important reality about teens who have been sexually abused is that many of them (*especially girls*) can become very histrionic and sexually promiscuous in their behaviors. Such girls are neither shy about their sexuality, nor do they have feelings of guilt and shame, such as walking around with poor dress and hygiene and/ or not wanting to associate with males. To the contrary, these girls have learned that by being flirtatious, they can attract the attention of men and get their needs met, whether these needs be physical, monetary, emotional or all three. Many use sex for monetary and material gain. They don't necessarily become prostitutes, but they will build a sexual relationship with a man in order to conn him out of money, a place to stay and material gifts. In short, this allows them to feel in control. This is especially true of girls who were victims of complex sex abuse. Complex sex abuse happens when the same people or group of people has repeatedly sexually abused a person over a long period of time.

During my foster care days, I fostered several girls between the ages of 10 and 15 who would dress in a manner that would put Marilyn Monroe to shame, turn the head of any man in the room and could also rewrite the Karma Sutra. Such girls are also prone to sexually acting out behaviors. They are very "touchy feely" with guys. They will crawl into the bed of any guy, even without his consent. I have even known of younger girls who have walked up to grown men in public and grabbed their crotches. The sad part is that such girls are very hard to redirect.

But isn't it normal for teenage girls to be attracted to guys and want to sit close to them or flirt with them?

Generally speaking, yes, but the difference is this. Normal teenage girls will be selective in terms of wanting to be close to a guy. They will have a crush on a certain guy (*or maybe two*) and want to flirt and get close to that guy. A girl who is sexually promiscuous as a result of sexual abuse will flirt and want to get close to any Tom, Dick or Harry who crosses her path....guys are an addiction.

Sexual Orientation

In today's world, it seems like every other day I am learning a new term associated with sexual orientation or gender identity. By the way, sexual orientation and gender identity are not one in the same (*more on this later*). Among the new terms that I have learned include pansexual, metrosexual, swingers and polyamorous; I know these terms have been around for a while, it just took me some time to "get with it." I am sure there are many more. The most recent term that I have heard is non-binary, which I understand to mean the person does not want to be thought of as either male or female, just a person... OK, this is fine.

In today's world, teens are bombarded with all sorts of varieties of sexual orientations and gender identities. I must clarify that although the terminology is new, these sexual orientations and gender identities are not new. They have always been a part of humanity throughout time. However, in today's world, society is more accepting of such lifestyles; hence, the terminology has been born. Sometimes I feel like all of this terminology is like a Sunday lunch buffet at a major restaurant chain... so many goodies to try. Although, I must clarify that a buffet implies choice and sexual orientation and gender identity at an innate level is not a choice. I will get back to innate sexual orientation and gender identity, shortly.

Based on clinical observation over the past decade, many of my teen clients, especially girls (*and I do see many boys as well*) do seem to be trying on different sexual orientations and gender identities (*as if they are the latest clothing fad*) devoid of their innate orientation and gender. My experience is that some such teens are trying to shock their parents, create a unique self in some way, fit in with a certain crowd and/or seeing if it clicks with them, among several other reasons. If indeed it is just a fad, it will pass. On the other hand, some teens are innately homosexual and others innately have gender dysphoria. If this is innate, it isn't a choice.

Here are the common terms associated with sexual orientation and gender identity.

Sex: The gender you were born as, either male or female.

Gender: The gender you identify with, male, female, both or neither.

Polyamorous: Someone who enters intimate relationships with more than one partner simultaneously.

Pansexual: Someone who dates people for their personality rather then their looks or gender.

A-sexual: A person who does not have any interest in engaging in sexual activity with anyone of any gender.

Metrosexual: A heterosexual male that has a lot of feminine qualities and strong anima energy *(meaning female energy)*; however he is not homosexual.

Trans-sexual: A person who identifies him or herself as being the opposite gender, usually he or she will dress and act as such.

Trans-gender: Is a person who has undergone an operation to become the opposite gender.

Non-binary: A person who does not relate to or identify as either gender; they do what makes them happy and don't let society dictate what is appropriate based on gender.

Gender Fluid: A person who identifies as being both genders.

Transvestite: A person who dresses as the opposite gender but still identifies as being the gender he was assigned at the time of conception.

Cisgender: A person who identifies as his assigned gender at the time of conception.

Fish:. A woman who prefers to have sexual relations with another woman (*a lesbian*) or a drag queen (*a man who dresses as a woman*) who is so convincing that he appears to be a biological woman.

Let's begin with sexual preference; we will come back around to gender identity later.

People are born into the world with an innate sexual preference; the same way people are born into the world as being innately left or right handed. Most people are right handed and very few people are innately ambidextrous. Likewise, people are born into the world being innately heterosexual or homosexual, most people are heterosexual and very few people are innately bisexual. When it comes to innate sexual orientation, we are who we are. There is no hocus pocus, magic wand or even a holy book that can change our innate sexual preference. Empirical research has proven that such actions are often psychologically damaging to the individual. Just as heterosexuals do not wake up one day (*or suddenly meet the right person of the same sex*) and change his or her orientation, neither do homosexuals.

Assuming that you are heterosexual (*and it is perfectly fine with me if you are not*) imagine, just for a moment, that homosexuality is what is considered universally conventional and acceptable to all. Now, imagine that you are being asked to change your orientation to homosexuality and fall in love and be sexual with a same sex partner. What feelings does this thought awaken within you? If you are like the overwhelming majority of heterosexuals, the thought is not very appealing. Well…. this is the same feeling which comes over homosexuals trying to imagine themselves in a heterosexual relationship. **It doesn't work…I rest my case.**

It always saddens me when someone believes he cannot be authentic about his sexual orientation and lives a suppressed sexual life or even a double life. I remember several years back, when I was getting my hair styled at a salon in Kuala Lumpur, which is where I have resided for many years. I was reading a magazine, *Malaysian Women's Weekly,* a magazine written and published in Kuala Lumpur. On the front cover was the title of one of the articles, *"I have slept with over 120 men; one of them might be your husband."* My first, immediate thought was what woman has the time to sleep around with over 120 men? I don't even have time to sleep with my husband (*enough on that subject*). So, I eagerly turned to the article hoping that the author would enlighten me with some of her time management and organizational skills. I mean, even "kept women" have schedules: hair appointments, afternoon teas, shopping, dress fittings, overseeing domestic staff; but… this woman had time to sleep with over 120 men… **WOW**! I couldn't wait to hear about it.

Well… to my surprise, I found that a local Malaysian homosexual man wrote the article. He was not married and obviously had a very active sex life (*to say the least*). The purpose of the article was to share with the public (*women especially*) how common it can be for homosexual men to get married, have children and put up this façade of being heterosexual, only to then have extra-marital affairs with homosexual men (*I assume they are homosexual*). How sad this is for not only the men who can't be authentic but also for the wives and children to whom they are lying. I believe that it is fair to say that (*in all likelihood*) there are also homosexual women doing the same. This is a perfect example of living the false self, as we've previously discussed…need I say more? I must say that innate homosexuality **is not a choice**. I have known many innate homosexuals and with each and every one of them, if it were a choice, they would choose to be heterosexual… **case closed.**

Below is what I have learned about human sexual orientation based on empirical research and clinical observation. For more in-depth, up-to-date empirical research on human sexuality (*both conventional and non-conventional*) consult the Johnson and Kinsey website. The website address is (**www. kinseyinstitute. orgresearch**).

The following is summarized from my first book, *Understanding and Caring for the Hurt Child.*

Innate Homosexuality: This is the person's natural sexual orientation. Simply put, innate means we are born that way and it is permanent. These people were born homosexual and will always be homosexual. See comments above about trying to change someone's innate sexual preference… **The End.**

Experiential Homosexuality: This can be typical of early teenagers who are curious about what it is like to be sexually intimate. They experiment with kissing and touching their friends of the same gender and age. If the teen is not innately homosexual, engaging in such activity will not cause him to become homosexual. Nine point nine times out of ten, after a couple of times of such experimentation, the teen will no longer care to experiment. He has been there and done that.

Reactive Homosexuality: Based on my professional and social experience, this is more typically found in women. I have never known a man to make such a choice based on abuse; however, this is not to say that such a man does not exist. Sometimes women who have been repeatedly abused by men choose to seek out romantic relationships and physical intimacy with other women. This is where they feel safe. This can be either temporary or permanent; however, the fact remains that it is a lifestyle of choice. The woman does not become innately homosexual. Again, innate means that someone was born that way and it is permanent.

Circumstantial Homosexuality: This occurs when what is the "natural tendency" is forbidden or not accessible, the "unnatural tendency" often prevails. This often happens when a heterosexual person is isolated from the opposite sex over an extended period of time, such as prisoners or teenagers in same sex boarding schools. However, not all people who become isolated in same sex institutions engage in same sex sexual relations. It is an individual choice made by the individual. These people easily and naturally revert back to heterosexual relations once they are out of same sex institutions. Again, such people do not become innately homosexual. They are merely getting their sexual needs met in the only way that is available to them at the time. Remember, we are sexual beings.

Baranovich, D. Understanding and Caring for the Hurt Child, Pearson, Singapore.

Gender Identity

I have found that many people confuse gender identity with sexual preference. They are not the same. Sexual preference is the gender with which you desire to have intimate, physical relations. Gender identity is the gender you "feel" you are - male, female, both or none of the aforementioned.

So, how is this different from homosexuality?

For example, a male can be homosexual; however, he feels very much like a male. He does not feel like he is a female. Many homosexual men are quite the macho men, working out at the gym building their biceps, playing center on the community basketball team and growing beards. They don't feel like a woman trapped in a man's body. The same is true for homosexual females, many of whom have long hair and paint their fingernails and toenails.

On the other hand, there are males who feel like they are females and females who feel like they are males. Again, this is innate. The person is born this way; it is not the result of being forced to wear a dress by his psychotic aunt or the result of being allowed to play with dolls (*if a male*) or cars and trucks (*if a female*) during one's pre-school years. Such a male who feels like a female cannot be considered homosexual because when a female desires physical relations with a male, this is considered heterosexual. The same is true for the female who feels like a male.

Now, there are also cases whereby gender dysphoria is comorbid with homosexuality. Meaning, a male can feel that he is a female and also be sexually attracted to other females. He (*she*) would then be a lesbian. The same would hold true for a woman who feels she is a male and is also attracted to other males.

The Clinical Term used in the DSM – V is Gender Dysphoria, which was formerly called Gender Identity Disorder in the DSM – IV

The DSM – V (American Psychological Association, 2013) explains the criteria for Gender Dysphoria for both adolescents and adults as follows:

A marked incongruence between one's experienced/expressed gender and his assigned gender, of at least six months duration, as manifested by two or more of the following indicators:

1. A marked incongruence between one's experienced/expressed gender and primary and/or secondary sex characteristics (or, in young adolescents, the anticipated secondary sex characteristics).

2. A strong desire to be rid of one's primary and/or secondary sex characteristics because of a marked incongruence with one's experienced/ expressed gender (or, in young adolescents, a desire to prevent the development of the anticipated secondary sex characteristics).

3. A strong desire for the primary and/or secondary sex characteristics of the other gender.

4. A strong desire to be of the other gender (or some alternative gender different from one's assigned gender).

5. A strong desire to be treated as the other gender (or some alternative gender different from one's assigned gender).

6. A strong conviction that one has the typical feelings and reactions of the other gender (or some alternative gender different from one's assigned gender).

So now, in today's world where all teens are very familiar with the above and also live in a time when such alternative gender identities are accepted (*in many places of the world at least*) it isn't uncommon for teens to experiment with different takes on gender identity when in fact they are innately the gender that they were assigned (*cisgender*) at the time of conception. The "trying on" is merely their false self trying to be unique and in search of a sense of self.

What does all of the above mean for mentors of hurt teens?

Often times teens will bring up the subject of their sexual orientation and/or gender identity; especially when they are feeling that their sexual orientation is or might be something other than heterosexual and/or feeling that they are not the gender that they were assigned at conception. When such conversation is brought up, the mentor merely listens and explains, "Adolescents is a time when we discover who we are as sexual beings and it is very normal to have such wonders, curiosities and questions. We all come to know our true sexual orientation and gender identity by the time we are adults."

If your mentee asks you if you believe that it is right or wrong to be this way or that way just say, "I am not judgmental. I can assure you that I like you for who you are. If you feel you need help with this, I can help find a qualified person." If the conversation continues, just be there to empathetically listen. If the teen says that he or she is homosexual and wishes he were a boy or she were a girl, say, "I am OK with this; I like you just the way you are." Time will tell if your mentee is saying this as a test to see if you will be judgmental or shocked by the disclosure, or if he really just want to be authentic with you. Another reason the teen might be mentioning this is because he needs to talk it out. If this is the case, say "I am happy to listen. However, if you feel you need help on your journey, I can help you find a qualified professional."

VERY VERY IMPORTANT

Speaking of qualified professionals, it is a very good idea for mentors to have a complied list of various different types of professionals and resources on hands at all times. It is also very important to go and meet the professionals and source out the resources before you recommend them. Websites, as well as other types of advertisements, can be very deceiving.

Dating

The adolescent years is a big time for dating in most cultures. They will usually talk to mentors about the people whom they are dating or hope to date. Just be open-minded and listen. Help the teen explore what is a good, safe date and what can be dangerous.

What is a good, safe date?

A good safe date…

- asks you where you would like to go and considers what you would like to do. He does not insist that you go here or there or do this or that;
- picks you up at your home, meets your parents and respects what time your parents ask that you be home;
- is honest about where you are going, whom you'll meet there and what you will be doing when you get there;
- respects the laws and curfews of your town and follows them accordingly.
- doesn't drink and drive; better yet, doesn't drink at all because he is underage;
- doesn't harass you physically in any way;

- doesn't ask you to give him or lend him money;
- doesn't get jealous of your other friends; he welcomes you to spend time with them as well;
- doesn't get jealous if you have other friends of the opposite sex (*or same sex if this is a homosexual relationship*);
- doesn't insist that you wear certain clothes or act a certain way when you are out together in public (*or in private for that matter*);
- calls you the next day if he says that he will;
- returns your calls and text messages and doesn't play "hard to get" games;
- doesn't force aspects of his culture or religious beliefs on you when you are not interested, or he knows that they don't suit you. If such beliefs are that important to him, he should seek out a similar person to date;
- is not secretive about who he is or where he is;
- is perfectly OK if you just want to be friends.

I believe this covers the subject. Please remember that hurt teens are very vulnerable and even though we help them become aware of the above, they are still likely to fall victims of people who do not follow the above. After all, so do adults; hormones can easily cloud our better judgment. Now, let's not forget that we are in the 21st century and the teen's we help know of no other century. Hence, there is the ever-pervasive issue of social media. It is important to help our teens realize the risk of meeting people on line.

It is important to remind our teens that...

- people are not always who they say they are;
- such people remain strangers until you come to know them off line and know of other people who know them;
- there is nothing wrong with checking up on the person to clarify if he is who he says he is through the proper authorities and channels;
- whenever we write something on line or do something on line, it can easily become public domain (*I believe this is called going viral; am I in the 21st century yet?*);
- when going to meet someone whom you met on- line, always do so in a public place - **a very – Very – VERY public place** (*like...maybe... Times Square on New Year's Eve*);

- it is always good to also cultivate face-to-face, in person friendships with others.

Also, don't be afraid to show your teen true accounts of people who have been killed or taken advantage of by people whom they have met on line.

Self-reflective Questions:

1. What are your views on human sexuality and sexual preferences?
2. What morals did your family have about sexuality and sexual preferences? How did these affect your thoughts and feelings on the subject?
3. What were your feelings about your own sexual identity as a teen?
4. To whom could you speak about sex and sexual relations as a teen?
5. What are your experiences associating, working with or helping people whose sexual preferences or feelings of gender identity are different than the norm (*whatever normal is these days*)?
6. How do you feel about mentoring a homosexual teen?
7. How do you feel about mentoring a teen who has feelings of gender identity that are different from the norm... again, whatever normal is these days?
8. What are the local community services in your area that you could recommend a struggling teen to go to if such services are need?

Diana's Pearls of Wisdom – It is important to remember that each and every one of us is an innately special, unique and beautiful person. This is cause for celebration each and every second of every day.

CHAPTER TWELVE

Tying it all Together: Let's go to the Movies

I love to watch movies about real people in real life situations. I find that it is also a very good way to see many theories about human development in action. Below are several movies about adolescents that I find portray many of the theories that are relevant to teenage development. These are American movies, with the exception of one British movie, **Notes on a Scandal;** however, the themes and theories are universal. I am sure you can also find movies from your own culture, which portray the same themes and theories.

As you watch the movies, think about the different theories we have been discussing thus far, developing a sense of self (*false or true*), Maslow, Marcia, Payne, Bandura, Ericson, parenting and mentoring styles, vicarious living, attachment etc. You will find them all in the movies below. I didn't include a discussion section because not only would this add another 100 or more pages to this book, but I believe that you will find it is pretty straight forward. Also, some discussion questions are subjective and there are several correct answers. Also, most of the titles below are appropriate for you to watch and discuss with your mentee. Watching appropriate movies, which have a themes and messages that your mentee can relate to in some way, can be very therapeutic for your mentee.

Have Fun at the Movies and Don't Spill the Popcorn

The Pre-adolescent Years (10 – 12)

Movie One
Akeelah and the Bee (Lionsgate, 2006)

The protagonist, Akeelah, is an 11 - year old African American girl being raised by her single mother. Akeelah's father was killed in a drive by shooting a few years before the start of the movie. Akeelah is innately very bright; however, she is beginning to skip school with her friends and is also becoming an academic underachiever. Her English teacher recognizes that she is a gifted speller and encourages Akeelah to enter the school's spelling bee. The principal of the school asks Dr. Larabee, a university English professor who is also African American, to encourage Akeelah to go to the regional spelling bee. Akeelah is very reluctant at first, but she eventually begins intensive study sessions with Dr. Larabee. This journey takes Akeelah all the way to the national spelling bee. In preparation for the spelling bee competition, Akeelah develops new friendships and even becomes a role model for her family, friends and her entire community.

Discussion Questions to Ponder

1. Discuss Akeelah's Self- efficacy level in terms of Bandura's self-efficacy theory.
2. Discuss Akeelah's personal resources in terms of Ruby Payne's theory.
3. Ruby Payne's theory states that a person must have two things to make a permanent move from generational poverty to middle class. Does Akeelah have these two things? Explain.
4. Ruby Payne's theory also explains that people of poverty keep each other in poverty. Explain how this is portrayed in the movie.
5. Discuss Akeelah's relationship with Dr. Larabee and how it changes over time. What makes it change?
6. Discuss how Akeelah changes her playmates and her playground.
7. Discuss how Akeelah becomes a role model for her peers and her community.
8. How does Akeelah become a role model for her mother?
9. Discuss the parenting style of Akeelah's mother and how it changes during the course the film.

10. Discuss the parenting styles of the following parents.
    - Javier's parents
    - Dylan's parents
    - The boy who was cheating
11. How does Dylan's attitude toward competition change throughout the film? What does this say about his self-esteem and emerging sense of self?

If you enjoyed this movies, below are some other suggested titles you will likely enjoy. All of which portray the pre-adolescent stage of development. As you watch the following movies, continue to think about the emerging sense of self, as well as the other theories covered so far, including: Bandura, Payne, Marcia, Maslow, Erickson, Diana's parenting styles and good old attachment theory.

***Bridge to Terrabethia* (Walden Media, 2007)**
***Ramona and Beezus* (Fox 2000 Pictures, 2010)**
***Little Manhattan* (New Regency Pictures, 2005)**

The Early to Middle Adolescent Years (13 – 15)

Movie Two
***Thirteen* (Fox Searchlight Pictures, 2003)**

This is a true-life docudrama about a 13-year-old girl, who is desperately trying to be popular. However, she befriends the wrong friend. The girl this happened to in real life plays the part of Evie, the bad friend; however, in real life, she experienced what Tracy, the protagonist, experienced. The protagonist, Tracy, is a 13-year-old girl being raised by a single mother. Her mother runs a hair saloon business in her home. Her father is rarely available for Tracy and her brother. Tracy's mother is a compassionate soul who goes out of her way to help others in need, often times, at the emotional expense of herself and her children. Desperate for a sense of love and belonging, Tracy befriends a pretty, popular girl at school, Evie. However, Evie (*a sociopathic con-artist*) is herself without parents and full of vice. Evie shows Tracy a world of drugs, sex and theft. All of which lead to Tracy's demise when she realizes that Evie really isn't a good friend.

Discussion Questions to Ponder

1. Discuss the parenting styles of Tracy's mother and father.
2. Describe Tracey's mom, in terms of true vs. false self.
3. Describe Evie's guardian, in terms of true vs. false self.
4. Discuss the personality of Evie.
5. What role does Brook play as Evie's guardian?
6. Discuss Tracy's feelings about the lifestyle of her mother.
7. In what way is Tracey being abused by her mother.
8. Tracy's mother tries to please Tracy by buying her the pants that she wants and taking her to her friends' houses. However, Tracy continues to be rebellious. Why does Tracy continue to reject her mother?
9. How does Tracy's brother cope with the family situation?
10. Discuss Tracy's personal resources throughout the movie.
11. Discuss Tracey in terms of being bullied and Evie in terms of being a bully.
12. Discuss Tracey's attitude and issues about her mom's boyfriend.
13. What actually made Evie turn on Tracey at the end of the movie?
14. What type of help do both Tracy and her mother need at the end of the film in order to bond as teen and mother.

Movie Three
My Life as a House (Winkler Films, 2001)

This movie portrays the poignant journey of a man, George, who decides to tear down his small cottage home in a prestigious neighborhood and build a large house that exceeds the size of all the other houses on the block. This causes much disharmony between himself, his neighbors and even the city council. In the process of rebuilding his house, George manages to also rebuild his relationship with his oppositional teenage son, his ex-wife, his neighbor and most importantly himself.

Discussion Questions to Ponder

1. Describe and explain the relationship in terms of parenting styles and attachment theory between Sam and his father and Sam and his mother?

2. Describe and explain the relationship between Sam and his stepfather, Peter, and his stepbrothers, Ryan and Adam.

3. Describe and explain the relationship between George and his ex-wife, Robin. How does this change and evolve throughout the film.

4. What contributed to the Gothic appearance of Sam in the beginning of the movie? What is this saying about his sense of self?

5. What environmental factors contributed to Sam being involved in male prostitution?

6. What led Sam to help his father build the house?

7. What led Sam to change his appearance from Gothic back to a more conventional appearance?

8. What did Sam mean when he mentioned "I am nothing" as he was chatting with his father?

9. Describe the relationship between Sam and Allysa?

10. What does the fact that Sam likes to put on his headset all the time say about his character?

11. What made Sam attempt suicide in the beginning of the movie?

12. Discuss Sam's self-awareness in terms of personality, academics, social interaction and sexual orientation.

13. Sam's moral conscience changes from when he was involved with male prostitution and when he decided to give away the home that was built for the girl whom his grandfather hit during an accident. What about Sam's emerging sense of self brings on this change?

14. How might the relationship between George and Sam evolve if George had not been diagnosed with terminal cancer?

15. What is the significance of Sam jumping into the ocean towards the end of the movie?

16. Discuss the relationship between Sam and his mother at the end of the movie?

17. In terms of James Marcia's theory, where is Sam in terms of ego identity by the end of the movie?

18. What did Sam mean when he mentioned "Everything happens for a reason," when he was approached by a policeman and his neighbor, David?

19. Describe and explain the metaphor "Life as a House" in relation to this movie? Think along the lines of renovation.

Movie Four
Before and After (Caravan Pictures – 1996)

The lives of Carolyn a small-town doctor, and her artist husband, Ben, are greatly challenged when their son, Jacob, becomes the prime suspect in the death of a local teenage girl. This causes this affluent family to face much bias among their working class neighbors. Carolyn is determined to learn the truth about her son's involvement in the murder, while Ben is willing to protect his son at any cost, regardless of his guilt or innocence. Ben will even break the law himself. When Jacob finally tells his parents what happened the movie takes many surprising turns to the very end.

1. Discuss the mistake that the policeman made in the beginning.
2. Discuss the concept of "mob psychology" among the townspeople.
3. Discuss the theme of "family ties" through out the movie.
4. Discuss Jacob and Jude in terms of attachment to their parents.
5. Discuss Jacob and Jude in terms of sibling bonding.
6. Discuss Jacob in terms of Ruby Payne's six personal resources and Bandura's self-efficacy theory.
7. Compare and Contrast the parenting styles of Jacob's mother and father.
8. How might "the family's" situation been different if Jacob were also a "poor boy?"
9. Discuss Jacob in terms of true self vs. false self throughout the movie.
10. Discuss Jacob's family members (*Mom, Dad and Sister*) in terms of true vs. false self throughout the movie.
11. At any point in the movie, do you see Jacob as being a parentified child? Explain. *Hint, I do.*
12. Do you believe the judge was fair with Jacob in terms of the sentence he gave Jacob?
13. Discuss the personality style and intentions of the lawyer from both a personal and professional point-of-view.
14. What makes the family "feel" that they had to move?

Movie Five
Freedom Writers **(Paramount Pictures, 2007)**

Based on a true story, this movie is about the first year journey of Ms. G., a young, dedicated teacher in the racially divided city of Los Angeles. The inner-city high school, where Ms. G teaches English, has many hurt teenagers who have been labeled hopeless and incapable of learning. This only motivates Ms. G to work harder to build rapport with her students and understand their plight in life. Although she meets with much adversity from her fellow teachers and the school system, her fortitude prevails. By assigning reading and writing assignments that relate to the lives and experiences of her students, Ms. G. inspires her students to take an interest in their education and plan for their future.

Discussion Questions to Ponder

1. How does Ms. G enhance her student's affective domain through her teaching techniques? *The affective domain of education will be discussed in the next chapter.*
2. How does Ms. G enhance her student's social awareness?
3. Why are the students so unwilling to associate with anyone outside of their own ethnic group? Where does this intolerance come from?
4. Ms. G is the first teacher to show trust and respect for the hurt students at Wilson High. How does Ms. G. demonstrate this? What makes the students resistant to this?
5. Why is trust an import component of a teacher-student relationship in respect to the affective domain?
6. How do the classmates come to trust one another? How do reading and writing initiate this change?
7. Ms. Gies, the woman who hid Anne Frank in her attic during WWII, is a hero to Ms. G's students. What does Ms. Gies mean when she tells Ms. G's students, "You are heroes everyday"?
8. What makes Eva choose to "go against her people" during the trial? Do you think this was a good decision? Explain. What causes her family and friends to react the way that they do? *Refer to Ruby Payne's theory.*
9. In what way does Ms. G's classroom become a family for the students? *Remember Maslow's third level - Love and Belonging.*

10. Describe how writing in journals helps transform the lives of the students. How does writing "free" the students from their pain?

11. Most of he teachers at Wilson High do not dress in formal attire. Why do you think MS. G chooses to wear business suits and pearls to class? What impression does this make? How do clothes, accessories, and make-up affect how other people perceive us?

12. What might your dress and accessories say about you to hurt teens?

13. Why are honor students treated differently than the "at risk" students?

14. How did the students' overall experience of having Ms. G. as a teacher enhance their sense of self? *Think Ruby Payne.*

15. What is the most significant "message" you received from this movie about hurt teenagers?

Let's go deeper...

Imagine you are a mentor to one of the students in Ms. G's class. Which student would you like to mentor and what would be your plan of action? What do you believe makes you a "good fit" for this particular teen?

Movie – Six
Mask (Universal Pictures, 1985)

Rocky Dennis is an intelligent, outgoing and humorous 14-year-old boy who suffers from a facial deformity called Lionitis and has already outlived his life expectancy. His mother is a member of a motorcycle club and abuses drugs and alcohol at times. While Mom struggles to fight for Rocky's acceptance in the public school system, Rocky proves to be a highly accomplished student and is much respected by his teachers and classmates. Although Rocky, at times, endures ridicule for his appearance along with physical pain, he finds love and belonging with his mother's biker gang family and even experiences his first love with a blind girl.

Discussion Questions to Ponder

1. Discuss Rocky's sense of self?
2. How does Rocky's mother serve as his advocate.
3. Discuss Rocky as a person on a self-actualizing path according to Maslow's theory.

4. What makes it easy for the members of the biker gang to relate to Rocky?
5. Discuss Rocky's mother's parenting style. *Hint - this fluctuates.*
6. Discuss Rocky as a parentified child.
7. Rocky has an amazing "self- regulating" techniques when he is feeling either physical and/or emotional pain. Discuss these techniques.
8. How does Rocky's dream of traveling and collecting baseball cards serve as therapeutic tools for him.
9. Discuss Rocky's sense of autonomy and self-reliance.
10. What makes Rocky a good candidate to be a counselor at the blind children's camp?
11. How does Rocky grow emotionally as a result of working at the camp.

Below are more movie titles from the early adolescent stage of development As you watch the following movies, continue to think about the emerging sense of self, as well as the other theories covered including: Bandura, Payne, Marcia, Maslow, Erickson, Diana's parenting styles and attachment theory.

***Jeremy* (United Artists, 1973)**
***Ice Princess* (Walt Disney Pictures, 2005)**
***Fame* (Metro- Goldwyn- Mayer, 2009)** *This movie also includes the middle adolescent years.*

The Middle to Late Adolescent Years (16 – 18)

Movie - Seven
***Save the Last Dance* (Paramount Pictures, 2001)**

Sarah is a talented dancer who dreams of being accepted into Julliard upon high school graduation. She is an only child being raised by her single mother. Sara and her mother have a very healthy parent-teen bond. At the beginning of her senior year in high school, Sarah's mother is killed in a car accident. Sara now is sent to live with her estranged father in the ghettos of Chicago to finish her senior year of high school. She is the only white student in the school. She befriends a fellow classmate, Derrick, an intelligent African American, who is bound for medical school and his insightful sister, Chanelle. Together they share their love of dance and become strong support systems for each other.

Sarah begins to enter Derrick's culture without loosing her sense of self, which is a very true sense of self. Derrick encourages Sarah to audition for Julliard and fulfill her dream.

Discussion Questions to Ponder

1. Discuss the cultural identity of Sarah at the very beginning of the film.
2. Discuss the level of attachment between Sarah and her estranged father and how this changes throughout the movie.
3. Although Sarah simulates into her new cultural environment, she maintains her true sense of self. What does Sarah say and do that allows the viewer to know that she is maintaining her true sense of self.
4. At the very beginning of the film, Chanelle reaches out to Sarah as a friend and mentor. What about Sarah made Chanelle decide to befriend Sarah right away.
5. Discuss the advantages that Derrick and Chanelle have even though they are growing up in poverty? *Think Ruby Payne's theory.*
6. Where are Maliki and Nikki in terms of Marcia's theory of ego identity.
7. How do Derrick and Sarah begin to blend their cultures through dance?
8. Derrick and Chanelle are great role models for their culture; however, none of their peers seem to see them as such. What might this be about? Once again, think about Ruby Payne's theory.

Movie – Eight
The Emperor's Club – (Universal Studios, 2002)

The protagonist, Mr Hundert, is a dedicated and inspiring classics teacher who has devoted his life to teaching at a prep boarding school for boys. It is the mid 1970's when a new student, Sedgewick Bell who is the arrogant son of a powerful senator, joins his class and challenges Mr. Hundert's sense of justice and morality. In hopes of motivating Sedgewick and giving him the opportunity to excel academically, Mr. Hundert alters the grades so that Sedgewick will qualify to enter an annual scholastic contest. Mr. Hundert is very disappointed in the outcome; however, he gives Sedgewick an opportunity to redeem himself at the 25th year class reunion only to realize that Sedgewick's character has not changed.

Discussion Questions to Ponder

1. How does Mr. H. enhance his student's affective domain through his teaching techniques? *The affective domain of teaching will be discuss in the next chapter.*

2. Discuss Mr. H's leadership style according to Diana's five types leadership styles.

3. What is "character?" What do you think Mr. H means by his quote, "A man's character is his fate"?

4. How did Mr. H. succeed at enhancing his student's sense of self? *Think out the box with this one.*

5. Describe the influence that Sedgewick Bell has on the other boys. They see him as an idol. Mr. H. describes Sedgewick's influence as "hypnotic". What does he mean by this?

6. Did Sedgewick turn out like his father? Explain.

7. According to Diana's parenting, mentor and leadership styles, a person's parenting, mentoring or leadership style has a lot to do with a person's character. Explain Sedgewick's father's parenting style and how this affected Sedgewick's character.

8. Did Mr. H. make the right choice to raise Bell's paper grade? What was Mr. H. hoping for when he did this?

9. Did Mr. H. fail? Explain Mr. H's quote, "However much we stumble, it is a teacher's burden always to hope that with learning a boy's character might be changed; and so, the destiny of a man."

10. Mr. H. says, "It is not living, but living rightly that matters." What does that mean? Did Mr. H. "live rightly"?

11. Twenty-five years later, Mr. H. is asked to participate in a rematch of the Julius Caesar Contest. Although Mr. H. is retired, he chooses to host the contest. Why does he do this? What does he hope for? How is his hope both squashed and then renewed?

12. Why does Mr. H. return to teaching? What surprise is there for him? Why is this surprise significant in the life and teaching career of Mr. H?

13. Return to the quote "A man's character is his fate." How was Sedgewick's character his fate? How was Mr. H.'s character his fate?

14. Think about Martin's sense of self. What about his sense of self allows him to be forgiving of Mr. H?

15. When Sedgwick is in high school, would he have been a good candidate for the mentor program? Explain

Movie – Nine
Dead Poet's Society (Touchstone Pictures, 1989)

The setting is the mid 1950's at a New England boarding school for aristocratic, high school boys. A new English teacher, Mr. Keating, uses unorthodox, student-centered teaching methods, which serve to challenge the old-fashioned traditions and standards of both the school's administration and the parents of the boys. As a result of Mr. Keating's inspirational teaching and the rapport he builds with the students, one student in particular is able to discover his innate talent and interest. As a result, this challenges the student's father's hopes and dreams for his future. This comes at great personal expense to this student, the other students and Mr. Keating. However, many of the students have grown from this experience.

Discussion Questions to Ponder

1. Why does Mr. Keating refer to himself as Captain? What is a captain's role?

2. Discuss Mr. Keating in terms of his leadership style according to Diana's five types of leaders.

3. How did Mr. Keating acknowledge the "affective domain" of education. *Again, the affective domain of teaching will be discussed in the next chapter.*

4. Discuss elements of Marcia's four ego states of identity status throughout the film in terms of the students, Mr. H, administration and the parents.

5. Discuss elements of the following as portrayed in the film:
   a. false self
   b. true self
   c. vicarious living
   d. emotionally battered wife

6. How was the theme of "scapegoating" portrayed throughout the film. What part does "tradition" play in the scapegoating theme?

7. How was the theme of "scapegoating" portrayed throughout the film. What part does "tradition" play in the scapegoating theme?

8. What is "Nuwanda" really all about? *Think sense of self.*

9. At the end of the movie as Mr. Keaton was leaving, some of the boys stand on their desks and clap while other boys remain seated. What does this tell you about the two groups of boys in terms of true vs. false sense of self.

Movie Ten
The Blind Side (Alcon Entertainment, 2009)

This film is based on the true story of Michael Oher, a homeless, African American teenager. He has drifted in and out of the school system for years when Leigh Anne and her husband, Sean, take him into their family as a legal foster child. His foster parents quickly discover Michael's protective instincts. This, along with his tremendous size, makes him a great candidate for the high school football team. With the unconditional love and fortitude of his foster family, teachers and tutors, Michael realizes his potential as both a student and a football player. In real life he becomes a member of the American Football Hall of Fame.

Discussion Questions to Ponder

1. Describe Mike from the view point of Bandura's self-efficacy model once he moves in with Le Anne and Sean.

2. Notice at the beginning of the movie when Le Anne asks Mike if he wants to live with them, Mike answers, "I don't want to live anywhere else." Notice, he doesn't merely answer, "Yes, I want to stay here." What might this be about? *Think attachment theory.*

3. Describe Le Anne's character. What are some examples of how she maintains a true sense of self in the face of the adversity she receives from the other women in her community when she decides to foster Mike?

4. Do you believe Le Anne was only thinking about herself when she wanted Mike to go to college and play football? Explain.

5. Where would you say Mike fits in with Marcia's identity status theory at the time he graduates?

6. Think about Le Anne and Sean's biological children, what about their upbringing makes them so patient, open and loving to Mike? *Think attachment theory.*

7. Toward the end of the movie, Mike questions his foster mom's intentions of why she was working so hard to get him into a certain university via a place on the football team. What makes Mike confused about his mom's intentions? *Think about* Mike's early programming.

Movie Twelve
Homeless to Harvard (Lifetime Movies – 2003)

Based on a true story. Liz Murray is a young girl who is taken care of by her drug-addicted father and mother. Her mother, who is also schizophrenic, moves back in with her father and takes Liz with her. To avoid living with her abusive grandfather, Liz begins to live on the streets, begging for money. When her mother dies, Liz (*at the age of 15*) decides to finish high school while living on the streets. Liz hides from authorities until her 18th birthday to avoid becoming a ward of the state. The one advantage that Liz has in her world of total poverty is an innately high IQ. She manages to finish four years of high school in two and a half years and is awarded a scholarship to Harvard University.

Discussion Questions to Ponder

1. What were Liz's motivating factors?
2. What were Liz's six personal resources?
3. Where is Liz in terms of Eric Erickson's theory of psychosocial development?
4. Where is she in terms of Maslow's hierarchy of needs? *She is a bit different when thinking of her in terms of this theory.*
5. Where is she in terms of Marcia's identity status, ego state?
6. What big gift does Liz have that is of tremendous help to her?
7. Where is Liz's friend, Chris, in all of the above?
8. Discuss Liz as a prettified child.
9. Discuss Liz in terms of true vs. false self.

10. At what point does Liz put herself before others to her own advantages? Think in terms of her sister, Lisa and friend, Chris.
11. Discuss how Liz changes playmates and her playground.
12. Compare and Contrast Liz to Akeelah (*Akeelah and the Bee*) in terms of advantages and disadvantages in life.

Movie - Thirteen
Here on Earth (Fox Pictures, 2000)

This movie is not based on a true story. Kelley Morse is an arrogant, affluent high school student who likes to party. Normally, he would never have crossed paths with the residents from a small town near his up-scaled private school. However, one night he decides to show off his new car by racing against a local boy, Jasper. Kelly and Jasper crash their car into a diner, destroying it. The courts sentence both boys to spend their summer rebuilding the diner. Kelley falls in love with the owner's daughter. This experience allows Kelley to evaluate himself, his culture, his goals and the world around him in a whole new light.

Discussion Questions to Ponder

1. Think of the self-awareness levels of Kelley, Samantha and Jasper in terms of personality, social achievement and identity achievement.
2. Describe and explain the parenting styles and interactions between:
   a. Samantha and her parents
   b. Kelly and his father
   c. Jasper and his parents
3. What caused the fight in the restaurant between Kelly and Jasper in the beginning of the movie?
4. Why was Kelley called and labeled as 'Richie Rich'? Was this fair?
5. What motivated Kelley and Jasper to continue racing until they damaged Samantha's restaurant?
6. What was the reason for Kelly and Jasper's punishment?
7. What might have been Kelley's childhood experiences based on how he is as a teenager? *Discuss bonding and attachment.*
8. Discuss the relationship between Jasper and Samantha throughout the movie?

9. What might be the reason for Kelley giving the 'graduation speech' alone in the forest?

10. What made Kelley become socially withdrawn from the rest of the community in Putnam?

11. What attracted Kelley and Samantha to each other?

12. What were Samantha's talents, interests and proclivities in this movie?

13. What made Kelley tell Samantha to get out of the bathtub?

14. What do you think happened to Kelley's mother…because?

15. How did both Samantha and Kelley come to accept the fact that Samantha was dying of cancer?

16. What made Kelley leave Putnam and then return again?

17. Discuss both Kelley and Samantha's sense of self at the beginning of the movie and their sense of self at the end of the movie?

Movie – Fourteen
A Walk to Remember (Pandora Films S.A., 2002)

Based on a novel by Nicholas Sparks, this movie is set in a small town in North Carolina. This movie portrays the journey of a high school boy, Shane, who seems to be heading down the wrong path in life. When the school principal insists he tutor some underprivileged children on the weekends and participate in the school play as a consequence for vandalizing school property, he falls in love with a studious, religious schoolmate whom many of his cronies scorn. Throughout the movie, the two of them develop an inspirational relationship, which leads both of them to discover deeper truths and meaning in life.

Discussion Questions to Ponder

1. Describe and explain the relationship between Landon and his mother in terms of parenting styles and attachment theory.

2. Describe and explain the relationship between Landon and his father in terms of parenting styles and attachment theory.

3. Describe and explain Landon's experiences as he tutors a young boy and participating in a play.

4. What causes Landon to behave differently toward Jaime when his friends are around at the beginning of the movie? *Think true vs. false self.*

5. What causes students at school to believe that Jamie is strange? Is she strange?

6. What are the talents, interests and proclivities of Jamie and Landon in this movie?

7. What role did Jamie play in Landon's evolving true sense of self?

8. How was the relationship between Jamie and her father in terms of parenting styles? How does this change throughout the movie.

9. In one scene Jamie's dad asks, "Do you care about God's opinion?" Jamie replies, "I think God wants me to be happy," What did Jamie mean by this reply? *Think sense of self.*

10. What made Jamie's father finally allow Landon to date his daughter?

11. Compare and contrast the parenting styles of Jamie's father towards Jamie and Landon's father towards Landon.

12. Think of the self-awareness of Jamie and Landon in terms of personality, school, social interaction, and identity achievement.

13. How did Jamie and Landon inspire each other throughout their relationship?

14. How was Landon's relationship towards his father at the end of the movie?

15. In what aspect was Landon an "angel" and a "miracle" to Jamie in this movie?

16. What does it mean at the end of the novel when Landon says that he now believes that miracles can happen?

Movie - Fifteen
The Chosen (The Chosen Film Company, 1981)

Daniel is a Hasidic Jewish teenager growing up in New York during WWII. While playing a game of baseball with the Orthodox Jewish high school, Daniel injuries a boy, Reuven, from the other team. Usually the boys from each team never associate with each other beyond playing baseball. Despite the fact that their fathers take opposing positions in the debate over whether or not to establish a secular Jewish state in Palestine, Reuven and Daniel become very close friends. The movie also focuses on Daniel, who is very gifted intellectually and has total recall. Danny wants to study psychology in a secular university; however, he is being pressured by his father to follow the family tradition (*which was established many years ago*) to become a Hasidic

Rabbi. Although this movie is set in the 1940's, the plot would be very much the same today in the 21st center. Hasidic Jewish people remain isolated within their own community.

Discussion Questions to Ponder

1. Discuss the Hasidic Jewish Faith (*Daniel*) to the Orthodox Jewish faith (*Reuven*) as you understand it.
2. Discuss isolation of the Hasidic Jewish faith. How does this tie in with parenting styles?
3. Discuss the emerging friendship between Daniel and Reuven. How does each teenager grow by being open to someone from a different culture?
4. Compare and Contrast the parenting styles of Daniel's father and Reuven's father.
5. Discuss the silence between Daniel and his father. Considering the culture, explain this from the viewpoint of child abuse.
6. Discuss both Daniel and Reuven's sense of self-efficacy.
7. Discuss both Daniel and Reuven in terms of Marcia's identity states.
8. Discuss Daniel's emerging sense of "true self."
9. What part does Daniel's mother play in his life?
10. How does Daniel's father become more enlightened throughout the movie? What eventually leads Rabbi Saunder's to give his son his blessing to study secular psychology?

Let's Go Deeper...

Compare Rabi Saunders's political ideology to David Malter's (*Reuvin's father*). At times, each father feels threatened by the other's views. At other times, each father displays strong respect for the other. How are the two men different from one another, and how are they are similar? How can they both dislike and respect one another at the same time? Which father do you believe has achieved a true sense of self? Have they both achieved a true sense of self? Explain.

Movie – Sixteen

White Oleander **(Warner Brothers, 2002)** - The movie begins when the main character, Astrid, is in her early teenage years and goes through her middle teenage years by the movie's end.

White Oleander chronicles the life of Astrid, a young teenager who journeys through a series of foster homes and a group youth shelter after her mother, Ingrid, goes to prison for capital murder; she killed her boyfriend. Ingrid even manages to control Astrid from behind prison bars. Set adrift in the world and exploited by all adults who are supposed to care for her, Astrid finally learns to take care of herself and confronts her mother. At the end of the movie, Astrid allows herself to love and moves in with her boyfriend. Astrid also comes to realize that like the white oleander flower, her mother is dangerous and beautiful.

Discussion Questions to Ponder

1. Discuss Astrid's mother's parenting style.
2. Discuss how every adult who becomes her caregiver (*yes, including Claire*) abuses Astrid.
3. Unlike in the movie, in the book, it is very clear that Astrid has a physical affair with Ray, Star's live-in boyfriend. Where does this "need'" come from in Astrid's? *This goes deeper than the fact that she never had a father.*
4. Why does Astrid cut off her hair after the fight at the group home? *Think true vs. false self.*
5. What is the turning point of Astrid's relationship with her mother?
6. Why does Astrid choose Rena as a foster mom and not the "nice" couple?
7. Discuss Astrid as a "chameleon." Notice the colors change and her style of dress changes every time she moves to a new place to live.
8. Discuss the symbolism of the White Oleander, which is a poisonous flower (*it's dangerous and beautiful*).
9. Does Astrid's mother really let her go in the end? Explain.
10. At the movie's end, Astrid is 18, what would you say is her identity status based on Marcia's theory. Explain.

Movie - Seventeen
School Ties **(Paramount Pictures, 1992)**

Set in post WWII New England, David, a high school senior from a working class family, receives a football scholarship to a prestigious prep school for boys. David feels that he must hide the fact that he is Jewish from his classmates and teachers because he fears that they may be anti-Semitic. Being a very talented football player, David quickly brings the loosing team to championship status and becomes the big man on campus. When his classmates discover that he is Jewish, his worst fears come true. His friends turn on him and his girlfriend breaks up with him. However, David's integrity wins in the end.

Discussion Questions to Ponder

1. Discuss the relationship that David seems to have with his father at the beginning of the movie.
2. Discuss how David was the victim of cultural stereotyping.
3. Discuss the concept of "mob psychology" in the movie.
4. Discuss Dillon's personality. How might this be a result of "dictating parents."
5. Discuss how the school system is abusing the students overall.
6. Compare and Contrast David and Dillon in terms of true self vs. false self.
7. What might the advantages be if David had told everyone he was Jewish from the very beginning? What might be the disadvantages?
8. What is meant by the line "Just because you are accepted doesn't mean you belong."
9. Discuss David as a hurt teenager.
10. Discuss the other boys in the movie as hurt teenagers. How are they hurt differently from David?

More movie titles from the middle adolescent stage of development

Continue to think about the emerging sense of self, as well as the other theories covered so far, including: Bandura, Payne, Marcia, Maslow, Erickson, Diana's parenting, mentoring and leadership styles and attachment theory.

The Breakfast Club (A&M Films, 1985)
Sixteen Candles (Channel Productions, 1984)
Footloose (Paramount Pictures, 1984 & 2011)
Summer of My German Soldier (High gate Pictures, 1984)
Mr. Holland's Opus (Hollywood Pictures, 1995)
For Keeps (TriStar Pictures, 1988)
Ice Castles (Columbia Pictures Corporation, 1978)
Ode to Billy Joe (Warner Bros, 1976)
Say Anything (Gracie Films, 1989)
Anywhere But Here (Fox 2000 Pictures, 1999)
The Upside of Anger (New Line Cinema, 2005).
Mean Girls (Paramount Pictures, 2004)
Girls Just Want to Have Fun (New World Pictures, 1985)

The Late Adolescent Years to Early Adulthood (19 – 21)

Movie Eighteen
Center Stage – (Columbia Pictures – 2000)

This is the story of 12 older adolescents who have begun an intense training program at American Ballet Academy in New York in hopes of attaining a spot with one of the professional ballet companies around the country. During their training program, they encounter tremendous physical and mental stress. Each of the trainees have personal issues, which stand in the way of their progress, including eating disorders, dictating parents and love affairs. Some endure better than others. Each dancer, in the end, acts in his own best interest and dreams prevail.

Discussion Questions to Ponder

1. How do the adolescents in this movie- Maureen, Eva, Jody, Cooper, Erik and Emily identify themselves in this movie? What are their similarities and talents beyond ballet?
2. Think of the self-awareness of Maureen, Eva, and Jody in terms of personality, school, social interaction, and identity status.
3. What is the type of parenting style portrayed by Maureen's mother based on Diana's parenting styles?

4. Discuss Bandura's self- efficacy model in the life of Maureen, Eva and Jody; explain which of the four aspects that helped them to achieve their self- efficacy.

5. How do Jonathan and Juliette (*the ballet instructors*) make comments on the abilities of their students? In what way does this help the students to improve themselves and in what way does it not?

6. What might be the reason for Maureen's to be bulimia?

7. Describe the type of friendship between Maureen and Emily, and Jody and Eva?

8. Was Maureen living from true self or false self? Explain.

9. Which character(s) portrayed their true selves in this movie? Explain.

10. What might be the reason Jody developed interest in modern dancing while she was still in the ballet academy? *Think true self and innate interests and proclivities.*

11. Describe the parenting style of Emily's mother in this movie?

12. Discuss the support systems for Maureen, Jody and Eva as they journey through this training program to achieve their goals.

13. Describe the leadership styles of Jonathan, Juliette and Cooper based on Diana's terminology.

14. What was the reason Maureen decided not to dance in the final performance?

15. At the movie's end, what was Maureen's mother projecting on Maureen? *Think vicarious living.*

16. How did Maureen acknowledge herself at the end of the movie?

17. What made Jody choose to become a principal dancer in Cooper's new company, rather than Jonathan's ballet company?

18. Which characters develop the most throughout the movie in terms of honoring their true selves and reaching identity achievement?

Movie - Nineteen
Goodwill Hunting (Miramax, 1997)

Will Hunting has a genius-level IQ but chooses to work as a janitor at Massachusetts Institute of Technology. One day, Professor Lambeau discovers Will solving a very difficult math problem. At this point the Professor decides to help Will reach his full academic potential and have a life beyond being a janitor. However, Will does not prove to be cooperative at first and is arrested for attacking a police officer. Professor Lambeau makes a deal with the judge to give leniency to Will if he promises to receive psychotherapy. This marks the beginning of Will being able to trust adults who want to help him and feeling a sense of love and belonging.

Discussion Questions to Ponder

1. Will is a classic case of an emerging young adult with attachment disorder. What caused this in Will's upbringing and how does it interfere with his present relationships. *Think attachment theory.*
2. What are the traits of attachment disorder portrayed by Will?
3. The therapist, Sean Mc Guire, begins the relationship with Will from a very clinical point of view. However, he becomes more of a mentor by the movie's end. Explain how this naturally evolved.
4. Discuss Sean as a wounded healer.
5. Sean asks Will to list the people he feels that he has real relationships with. What is Will's answer, and how does this relate to attachment disorder?
6. Discuss the similarities between the way Will's relationship with Sean evolves and the way his relationship with Skylar evolves.
7. What trigged Sean when he got angry at Will and held him up against the wall? Sean told Will that if he disrespected his wife again he would beat him up? This is very inappropriate behavior for a therapist. Explain.
8. What did reading and mastering subjects mean for Will psychologically? Why doesn't he transfer this knowledge to relating to people?
9. Notice that Will is very astute at reading people's characters. This trait is very typical in children and people with attachment disorder, even the ones who are not innately intelligent. Why is this the case?
10. Discuss Will at the end of the movie in terms of Bandura's self-efficacy theory and Ruby Payne's personal resources.

Movie - Twenty
American Chai (Dream Merchant Pictures, 2001)

College senior Sureel has always deceived his strict Eastern Indian parents in order to fit into American society. He is supposed to be majoring in pre-med;

however, he is really studying music and playing in a band. His father eventually discovers this, and Sureel gets kicked out of the band. Sureel also breaks up with his white girlfriend and begins dating another Indian American in order to appease his father. However, before Sureel realizes it, his parents are already making wedding plans.

Discussion Questions to Ponder

1. Describe and explain the parenting styles of Sureel's parents based on Diana's parenting styles.
2. What made Sureel hide most of the things about himself from his parents?
3. What kind of identity crisis was Sureel portraying in the beginning of the movie?
4. How did Sureel acknowledge himself as an individual?
5. What are the culture norms that Sureel's parents try to make him follow?
6. What are the rules that were established by Sureel's father towards Sureel in this movie?
7. Based on James Marcia's identity status, what is Sureel's level of identity status?
8. What are Sureel's and Maya's interests, talents and proclivities?
9. What made Sureel feel good about leaving the Fathead band?
10. Based on Bandura's theory on self- efficacy, what has or have been Sureel's support systems in pursuing his dream?
11. Describe the self- awareness of Sureel in terms of personality, college, social interaction and proclivities.
12. Describe the relationship between Sureel and Maya in terms of love and friendship.
13. Discuss Sureel's disposition when he was with each of the bands, Fathead and American Chai?
14. What made Sureel's parents decide that Maya is the right partner for Sureel?
15. How do the ideologies of marriage differ between Sureel and his parents?
16. Did Sureel honor his true self'? When and under what circumstances?

17. How did Sureel acknowledge himself during the South Asian Conference speech?

18. Where is Sureel based on Maslow's hierarchy of needs? Is Sureel on a path of self- actualization by the end of the movie? Explain.

19. How did both Sureel and Maya inspire each other?

20. What made Raju, Sureel's cousin, behave differently in America than he behaves in India? What does this say about true vs. false self?

21. What was the definition of "good life" as mentioned by Sureel's father when Sureel confessed the truth to his parents?

22. What led Sureel to confess and reveal the truth to his parents?

23. What led Sureel's father to change at the end of the movie?

Movie – Twenty-One
Boys Don't Cry; The Tina Brandon Story – (Hart-Sharp Entertainment, 1999)

This is the true story of Tina Brandon who was born a girl put knew that she was really a boy. Against her family's wishes, she began her transition into becoming a man in her late teenage years and renamed herself Brandon Tina. Brandon's life was cut short when he was brutally murdered as a result of a hate crime.

Questions to Ponder

1. Discuss the levels of self- awareness of Tina/Brandon, Lana and John in terms of personality, social interaction and sexual identity based on this movie.

2. Discuss Tina/Brandon in terms of true self vs. false self?

3. What were the disruptive behaviors portrayed by Tina/Brandon throughout this movie?

4. What might be the reason Tina/Brandon develops feeling towards woman?

5. Who were Tina/Brandon's circle of "true" friends?

6. How was the relationship between Lana and her mother in this movie? *Think parenting styles.*

7. How was Lana's family environment?

8. What might be the reason for John and Tom's disruptive behavior in this movie?

9. What was the reason for Tina/Brandon not appearing in the court for the proceeding?

10. How did the relationship differ between Lana with John, and Lana with Tina/Brandon?

11. What was Lana's proclivities? How did she plan to live her life based on her proclivities?

12. How did Tina/Brandon protect herself when Lana found her in the female jail?

13. How was the truth about Tina/Brandon revealed in this movie? What was Tina/ Brandon's trick after the truth was revealed?

14. What made Tina/Brandon hide the truth that she was raped and beaten by John and Tom?

15. Who appears to be the support system for Tina/Brandon in this movie …. because?

16. Describe the relationship between Tina/Brandon with Lana before and after the truth was revealed.

17. Why did John and Tom murder Tina/Brandon and Candace at the end of this movie? In your opinion, what might be the future for Cody, Candace's daughter, as she grows up?

More movie titles from the late adolescent stage of development

Continue to think about the emerging sense of self, as well as the other theories covered so far, including: Bandura, Payne, Marcia, Maslow, Erickson, Diana's parenting, mentoring, leadership styles and attachment theory.

The Competition (Rastar Films, 1980)
St. Elmo's Fire (Columbia Pictures Corporation, 1985)
Goodbye Columbus (Willow Tree See, 1969)
Urban Cowboy (Paramount Pictures, 1980)
Saturday Night Fever (Robert Stigwood Organization, 1977)
This Side of Heaven (Metro- Goldwyn- Mayer, 1937)
One-on-One (Warner Bros, 1977)
Henna Night (Yalla Film Company, 2009)
Flash Dance (Paramount Pictures, 1983)

Adults experiencing unfinished business from their adolescent years.

Movie – Twenty-Two
Notes on a Scandal (Fox Searchlight Pictures, 2006)

Barbara is a veteran teacher at St. George's High School. She senses a kindred spirit in Sheba, the school's new art teacher. Barbara, a lesbian, becomes very attracted to Sheba's beauty and charm, and the two become close friends. When Barbara learns of Sheba's sexual affair with one of her teenage students, Barbara begins to use the secret as a form of emotional blackmail against Sheba and the real drama begins.

Questions to Ponder

1. Think of the self-awareness of Barbara and Sheba in terms of personality, social responsibilities, social interaction and sexual orientation.
2. What is Barbara's projection toward Sheba?
3. What is Sheba's projection or impression towards Barbara?
4. How was the relationship between Barbara and Sheba in the beginning of the movie and how it develops throughout the movie until the end?
5. What was Barbara's perception and impression towards Sheba's family? What might this be about?
6. Explain the meaning behind this dialogue between Sheba and Barbara. Sheba says, "There is a difference between the life that you dream and the life as it is in reality." Barbara responds, "I know exactly what you mean".
7. What made Barbara think that she and Sheba can be lovers?
8. Discuss Sheba in terms of true vs. false self throughout the movie.
9. What led Sheba to have an affair with Steven? What was Sheba's projection toward Steven?
10. How did Steven make Sheba feel a sense of love and belonging.
11. What made Barbara think that her life with Sheba is similar? Do you agree with Barbara?
12. How was Barbara's response and reaction when Sheba was unable to attend to her cat dying? What causes Barbara respond so emotionally?
13. Discuss Sheba's response when she read Barbara's diary?

14. Near the movies end, Sheba puts on make-up in a strange way. What is this about?

Movie – Twenty –Three
A Walk on the Moon (Marimax Pictures, 1999)

The setting is in the summer of 1969 in upstate New York. The Vietnam War is breaking out, and there is the great concert in Woodstock. The protagonist, Pearl, is on summer vacation with her mother-in-law, teenage daughter and younger son at a holiday camp in Woodstock. Marty, Pearl's husband, is not with the family because he is busy working as a television repairman back home. Pearly, who became pregnant and married at 17, feels trapped in her life as a mother. When a charming, young clothes salesman comes to the campground to sell blouses, Pearly is swept off of her feet. Pearly and the salesmen begin a hot and steamy affair. They escape to the rock concert at Woodstock together; this has a great impact on Pearly's family life.

Discussion Questions to Ponder

1. What is the parenting style of Pearl and Marty towards their two children, Alison and Danny?
2. What did Pearl mean when she mentioned that she does not want Alison to end up being like her?
3. What made Pearl become attracted to the 'blouse man'?
4. What did Pearl mean when she stated, "I wish I hadn't had Alison so young?"
5. What might have been missing in Pearl's life that made her regress back to her younger adolescent life?
6. How did Alison's Mom, Grandma, and all residents at Dr. Folger's bungalow celebrate Alison's puberty?
7. Describe the relationship between Pearly and her mother-in-law. What type of parenting style does Pearly's mother-in-law use with her? Explain.
8. What might be the reason for Pearl not allowing Alison to go camping?
9. What was Pearl searching for in her relationship with the blouse man?
10. Describe Alison's relationship with Ruth (*her female friend*) and Ross?

11. What is the reason Pearl refused to listen to her mother-in-law when she stopped her from leaving the house to meet the blouse man?
12. What might be the reason for Alison to sneak out from the house?
13. Describe Pearl and her behavior while at the Woodstock festival.
14. Compare the level of bonding and attachment between Pearl and each of her two children.
15. According to Marty's mother, what was his adolescent year like?
16. In your opinion, who 'stopped' Pearl from doing things that she wanted to do?
17. What caused Pearl to return to Marty and let go of the blouse man at the end of the movie?

Below are suggested movie series, which depict the adolescent years

Don't forget to think about the emerging sense of self, as well as all the other theories covered so far, including: Bandura, Payne… you know the story by now.

Movie Series
Dawson's Creek (Outerbanks Entertainment, 1998- 2003)
The Gilmore Girls (Dorothy Parker Drank Here Productions, 2000- 2007)
7ᵗʰ Heaven (Spelling Television, 1996- 2007)
The Wonder Years (New World Television, 1988- 1993)
Eight Simple Rules (Touchstone Television, 2002- 2005)
Degrassi: The Next Generation (Epitome Pictures, Inc, 2001- 2015)

Self - reflective Questions

1. Which movie did you enjoy the most? What about the movie resonated with you?
2. Which movie did you not particularly enjoy? What makes you feel this way?
3. Did you find that your teenage years mirrored any of the teenagers in the movies lives?
4. Which teenager(s) from the movies do you believe you could help the most? In what ways?

5. If you were asked to play the part of any of the teenagers from the movies, which teenager would you like to play? What makes you want to play the part of this teenager?

6. Which teenage part would you absolutely not want to play? What makes you feel this way?

Diana's Pearls of Wisdom - The developmental plight of the hurt teenager is universal. North, East, South or West all teenagers on planet Earth are on a mission in search of **SELF**. It is guaranteed that they will find a sense of self. Let's hope they find a healthy, true sense of self.

CHAPTER THIRTEEN

Getting The Mentoring Process Started: Ice Breakers

First impressions mean a lot

Based on my decades of experience (*I'm beyond saying years now*), it always helps the rapport building process by taking an interest in something your mentee likes, even if you hate it. It also works best if you can do this in a spontaneous way. For example, if you notice your mentee has a certain sticker on his notebook, ask him about the sticker. Chances are that it is on his notebook because the sticker has some significance to him. If you notice he has on a certain brand of tennis shoes, ask him about the style. I have found that this spontaneous way works much better than if you ask your mentee to tell you something about himself or ask him what he likes.

I will never forget Valerie (*not her real name*). Valerie was a 17-year-old girl on probation from the juvenile detention center back in the early 1990's. Part of her probation agreement was to see me for a minimum of 10 counseling sessions. Typical of oppositional teens on probation, Valerie didn't want to come to counseling; she didn't trust any adult authority figure. She had had enough of adults trying to "reach" her. Valerie was tall and thin. Her hair was dyed an orange-red color. It was shaved on the sides and sticking up (*spiked)* at the top. She had a few small tattoos, several ear piercings in one ear, a dog collar with silver studs around her neck, and she was dressed all in black. Back then we referred to such a look as "punk rock." I believe the current term for this look today is "Goth." Our first two sessions were mostly silent. I first introduced my self to Valerie and reminded her why she was seeing me.

The short dialogue went as follows:

Me: Hi, Valerie, I am Diana, your assigned counselor.

Valerie: Hey (*looking down to the floor*).

Me: Would you like to have a seat (*She flops down on to the chair, slumped over*).

Me: As you know Valerie, it is part of your probation agreement for us to meet for at least 10 sessions.

Valerie: Yeah (*still looking down*).

Me: I am here to listen to whatever you feel comfortable sharing.

Valerie: Share what….you have my file….read it (*in a hostile tone of voice*).

Me: Yes, I have read your file, but I am interested in hearing your story from you.

Valerie: Yeah…. Yeah… nothing more to my story.

Me: I am ready to listen when you are ready to share.

There was total silence for the next 20 minutes.

Valerie: Do I have to stay the whole hour?

Me: Yes, you do.

There was silence for the remainder of this session and the second session….uhhh… an hour of silence can seem like a year.

I knew that I would find a way to get Valerie to "open up," but I also knew that it had to be (*or seem to be very authentic*). Then, it was the third session when Valerie gave me the perfect opportunity. I noticed her sitting in the waiting room with her head buried in a magazine.

I walked up to her, and we had the following dialogue.

Me: Hello, Valerie what magazine are you reading; may I have a look? *She abruptly hands the magazine to me with a frown on her face. I noticed that it was a Harley Davidson Motorcycle magazine.*

Me: Wow, Harley Davidson. This is the motorcycle that my friend's boyfriend has. I think it looks like this one. *I pointed to a picture of one of the motorbikes. This was not a true story by the way. For the first time, Valerie looked me in the face.*

The conversation continued as follows....

Valerie: You know about Harley Davidson Motorbikes? *She had an amazed look on her face.*

Me: Well, I don't really know about them. Just that my friend's boyfriend has one. You seem to know something about them." *Valerie begun to very enthusiastically tell me about them.*

Me: How about you come inside and tell me.

She came into my office. We sat side by side on the sofa; she spent the entire hour educating me about Harley Davidson motorbikes. I was interested solely for the benefit of building rapport. The next week she came in with another Harley Davidson magazine and began telling me about the accessories. I then used this as my point of entry into the therapeutic process.

The dialogue went as follows:

Me: I have an idea; can we both create our idea of the perfect Harley Davidson motorcycle helmet?

Valerie: Yeah, sure. *She had an enthusiastic tone to her voice.*

So...I got out the art paper, colors, paints, glitter, etc. and we went to work. She very carefully designed a glittery black helmet with orange, red and yellow fire flames. Mine was purple with pink and green flowers; yes, I know, quiet the contrast.

Me: What about your design is special for you?

She began talking about the fire flames being powerful. Then she talked about how fire has control. Valerie continued to explain that fire can be used in a good way or a bad way. She then began relating it to herself and her own experiences and feelings of being good, bad and powerful. This marked the beginning of our therapeutic journey. Valerie began to open up and trust. We finished our 10 sessions and she requested another 10.

I believe we ended with a total of 25 sessions. Valerie went back to school and attained her GED (Government Equivalency Diploma), began working part time at a motorcycle shop and eventually went to trade school for theatrical make up. To my knowledge, she stayed out of trouble.

I have learned so many things by entering the world of my clients. I have learned Bollywood dances, basketball shots, how to play chess (*which I swore I never would*) how to make friendship bracelets, fold origami paper into birds and stars, and many of the names of the Pokemon characters, hypebeast photography.... who knows what is next. I did this all for the purpose of developing rapport and entering the world of the child or teenager.

Now, let's remember, please. This is the 21st century, which equates with the world of gadgets. So, unfortunately, entering a teen's world might mean learning about some computer game he is enthusiastic about. I let this be OK for a very short time. Then I begin to take the teenager beyond the game. Such as, let's imagine that you do attain all the weapons needed to bring you to the highest level. What do you imagine will happen to the Kingdom once all bad men are eradicated? This will begin giving you insights into his value system. I never spend session time playing computer games with teenagers, even though this may be his current world. This is because we wouldn't be connecting with each other person-to-person; we would be connecting to the game. However, there are some computer programs, such as Sims Park, where you can design houses and things. I have engaged in this type of computer play because it allows for us to discuss options, make choices together and do something that is creative. However, I also begin to explore other non-gadget interests the teenager has...hopefully there is something. I also explain to the teen that this is our special time and I want to get to know him as a person.

Academics with Hurt Teenagers: Building Relationships

"Locate a Resilient Kid and you will also find a caring adult or several who have guided him."

Invincible Kids, *US News and World Report*, 2013

When it comes to hurt teenagers (*especially the ones from poverty*), the key to motivating him to take an interest in academics is to first build a relationship. Teachers, as well as other adults, are the enemy according to hurt teenagers. Teachers have said things to hurt teens such as you are lazy; you don't care; you never finishes assignments; you are hopeless, etc. So.....why should he care about academics? Motivating the hurt teen about anything begins with creating a relationship.

When hurt teenagers from poverty, who have made a permanent move to middle class, are asked, "How did you do it? The answer is 10 times out of 10 (*or at least 9.9 times out of 10*) about a relationship: a teacher, counselor, a coach, a church/temple/mosque/synagogue leader, etc. who took an unconditional interest in him as a unique individual.

The importance of the affective domain in the teaching and learning process.

Schools often send enormous amounts of time on teaching "achievement" and effective studying teaching strategies. They forget that of equal (*or of more importance*) is relationship building. In other words, the focus needs to also be on the affective domain of teaching.

We are all very familiar with the cognitive domain of teaching, meaning to enhance the student's ability to understand the subject matter being delivered. Furthermore, the teachers who do a "good job" will also help the student to see how the subject matter is related to and is useful in his day-to-day life. The affective domain of the teaching-learning process is enhancing the student's emotional development by enhancing his self-esteem and self-efficacy, as well as, making him feel that he is a capable, unique person. As a result of enhancing the student's affective domain, the student usually begins to enjoy the subject matter more. In short, through words (*and more importantly actions*) the teacher allows the student to know that **HE**, as a person, is more important than the subject matter.

Keeping an emotional bank account

Stephen Covey (1989) refers to this as an emotional bank account. He explains that when in a relationship both parties make emotional deposits and withdrawals into each other's bank accounts. The first step in building a relationship that is paramount is to make deposits into the relationship account. The fundamental core of relationships is one person interacting and relating to another.

Covey, S., *Seven Habits of Highly Effective People* (1989). Free Press, New York.

In education the relationships include, one student to one teacher, the student to each administrator then it is all the players on the team. This does not mean that the relationships between students and administrators do not have limits and boundaries. However, it is important that teachers and administrators honor each student as a unique individual, worthy of respect and care in order to establish a relationship that will enhance learning. Again, the emphasis must be placed on the **affective domain,** especially with hurt teenagers.

Making deposits with hurt teenagers; forget about withdrawals, at least initially.

Below are four suggested ways to make deposits into your mentee's account.

1.) Have an appreciation for your mentee's sense of humor and verbal expression. Criticizing or correcting his humor or vernacular is never recommended.

Example: Your mentee says "That lady has a fat ass; I wonder if she wants a burger with that shake."

Response that would hinder relationship building would be – "That is impolite, it is not appropriate to talk about other people in that manner; you shouldn't even be looking at her backside."

Relationship building response would be – "I see you are observant and notice woman's figures. What are some other things about people and places that you naturally notice?

2.) Respect what your mentee can't say or isn't willing to say about a person, people or situation in his life.

Example: Your mentee is trying to explain his relationship dynamics with his family. He says, "My father is so old school, and he just doesn't get how to treat women. He treats my mom like shit."

Response that would hinder relationship building would be - a very direct, closed questions, such as "Does your dad hit your mom?" or "What is your dad doing to your mom that makes you say this?"

Relationship building response would be "Yes, times are changing; unfortunately, some adults are stuck in the old ways. This can be very frustrating when we see people stuck in the old ways and because of this, others get hurt." By answering in this manner, you have let the teen know that you have heard, understood and empathize with his comment without probing. If the teen wants to share more at that time he will.

3.) Respect your mentee's station in life and his lifestyle; furthermore, be comfortable meeting him on his turf.

Example: Your mentee wants you to meet him at a playground in his neighborhood.

An Example that would hinder relationship building would be – insisting that the mentoring meetings be in some place in your middle class world.

Relationship building response would be - meeting him on his turf as long as you feel that you would be safe.

It has been my experience that hurt teens from poverty respect the middle class adults who are willing to go to their side of the tracks. This allows the teen to know that you don't think you are "too good" for his neighborhood. However, I must repeat, make sure that you are safe.

4.) Having a genuine awareness that your mentee will not be able to make plans about his future and set goals straight away. Concentrate on building rapport and trust in the beginning and allow your mentee to pace the process of planning and goal setting.

An Example that would hinder relationship building would be – on the first mentoring session asking your mentee to write down his goals and plan to achieve those goals. Goal setting is unfamiliar to the hurt teen. He wouldn't know where to even start with the process in a realistic way.

An Example that would help relationship building would be - spend several sessions entering your mentee's world, allowing trust and rapport to be built and also noticing his talents, interests and proclivities. Let goal setting and planning happen organically; it will, **PATIENCE.** In short, teen's who don't feel comfortable will shut down very easily. Remember, he doesn't trust you.

5.) Having an appreciation for your mentee's freedom of speech and personal expression.

For example, you are meeting your mentee at Starbuck's for a session and he comes dressed in dropped pants, which show the top of his boxer shorts, and he uses street vernacular during the conversation, such as "Man, this English teacher.....she be trippin. She wants us to read 30 pages of some book in one day. Man, I can't even read one page of that book. I never read that sort of English before. All these words, twas and hether to; what kinda language that be? Ain't no language I ever hear."

An Example that would hinder relationship building would be – commenting on his dress in a negative way, looking embarrassed to be seen with him and correcting his English.

An Example that would help relationship building would be – saying nothing about his dress or style of speech and engage him in a conversation about English, such as asking him what about English he has enjoyed in the past. Maybe talking about old style English and how it isn't so difficult once we understand the few words and expressions that are different. Ask if he would like to read some of the novel together. Let him decide. The fact that he is mentioning this means that he is looking for some sort of support in the matter.

When we understand the deposits that are valued by hurt teens, the relationship is stronger. **Support systems are networks of relationships.** A school system becomes a support system for the students when the school cares about the students, promotes student achievement (*both the cognitive and affective domain, as well as extra curricular*), being role models and insisting upon (*as well as nurturing*) appropriate behaviors.

PLEASE remember the ripple effect; we won't reach all students; however, just by making a difference in one in a 100 students, it will all add up. When I look back on my 35 years of teaching (*from nursery toddlers to PHD students*) what I remember the most are the relationships that were built. As a matter of fact, I cannot give you one example (*seriously, not as single one*) whereby I managed to help a student take an interest in the subject matter or understand the subject matter more without first building a relationship. In short…life is about relationships.

As for hurt teens from poverty, the primary motivation for their success will be in their relationships. Actually, the primary motivation for any teen's success is in their relationships; however, unhurt teenagers (*from whatever socio-economic class*) have positive relationships in place; hence, we forget about the powerful significance of relationships for the unhurt population.

What are the ways you can build relationships?

First and foremost it will be the way we verbally interact with people.

It's all in your voice. As the old saying goes, "It is not so much what you say, but how you say it." This means both the tone of your voice and the words used.

The Three Voices

Ruby Payne also discusses the three different voices we all use in our day-to-day lives. Everyone has three voices in his head at all times. These three voices are the child voice, the adult voice and the parent voice.

Payne, R. (2001). *A Framework for Understanding Poverty*, **Aha Press, Houston, TX.**

Based on my own clinical observation, people who have had to parent themselves, and perhaps parent others from a young age, often do not have an internal adult voice. One important fact to remember when mentoring hurt teenagers is that many of them are products of ghost parenting; hence they have had to be their own parents. Many times, they have also had the extra burden of parenting younger siblings and perhaps even their parents. Remember...the parentified child. Hence, hurt teenagers will have a child voice (*because their emotional age is still very young*) and the parent voice because they have had to boss people around to get their needs met.

The Child Voice

Although at times the child voice can be delightful and positive, the child voice is usually negative and annoying. It is defensive, victimized, emotional, whinny, negative and can be very antagonistic.

Common phrases from the child voice, both positive and negative.

The **negative child voice** is often used when times are tough and the teen feels powerless. The child voice can also be manipulative. On the positive side, the child voice is also playful, adventures and curious.

Common phrases from the **negative child voice** include:

- Stop hitting me
- You don't love me
- You took my pencil
- This sucks

- I hate you
- Everyone hates me
- It's your fault
- You made me do it
- I didn't do it, he/she/they did it
- Everyone hates me
- I am so stupid
- You are so stupid
- I am going to run away
- I am going to kill myself

The **positive child voice** is cheerful and full of excitement, wonder and curiosity.

Common phrases from the **positive child voice** include:

- Hey, look what I found
- Hey, look what I did
- I love you
- You are so pretty, smart, etc.
- Wow, I got it right this time

The Parent Voice

The parent voice is authoritarian, directive, judgmental, demanding and threatening. The parent voice also has a win-lose mentality. During conflict, the parent voice creates shame, guilt and self – doubt.

Common phrases from the **parent voice** include:

- You shouldn't or should do this or that
- That is wrong
- That is stupid, immature
- Act your age
- How many times must I go over this with you
- Stop being so lazy
- Life's not fair, so get used to it.

- You are good, bad, worthless, spoiled, selfish *(any judgmental word)*
- Do as I say, you will thank me some day
- I've been where you are; I know what's best
- Why can't you be like…..
- Here you go again; when will you ever learn

The **parent voice** is the disciplinarian. It takes the lead and gives orders. Teachers and coaches tend to use their parent voice when disciplining their students. This very much offends the student who is already using his parenting voice. The hurt teenager doesn't want to be parented, that is unfamiliar to him. Parents are never helpful and never know what is going on anyway.

When the teen is already a parent in some way, this causes him to be very angry. This causes fear in the student. Hence, the teen responds to hearing the parent voice by using either his parent voice or his child voice. When the teen uses his parent voice in this situation, he is seen as being disrespectful and gets in trouble. If the teen uses his child voice, he or she will feel helpless and at the mercy of the adult. Most often teens will use their parent voice because it is less frightening than feeling helpless. It is part of the false self. This is also a coping mechanism. Because resources are limited in poverty, there is no room to practice negotiation, which is the adult voice.

Then we have the **adult voice;** common expressions of the adult voice, include…

- Can we talk this over
- What might be causing this
- How can I help
- I know this is one of my shortcomings; I will work on it
- Sorry, that was my fault
- What do you think about…
- I forgive you, we all make mistakes
- Thanks for your support
- I appreciate your….

Notice that the **adult voice** is never critical or judgmental. Bonded parents, leaders and mentors consistently use their adult voice. It is always supportive and wants to work as a team to solve problems. The importance of the adult voice is that it serves as a negotiator. It allows for compromise, decision making and empathetic understanding of others. It is important to remember that people in poverty are in survival mode. Money and material goods are viewed on a day-to-day basis. Long term (*or even short term*) planning usually doesn't exist. Resources are limited; therefore, with limited resources comes limited choices. Choices promote thought, planning and negotiation. Where there is limited choices or no choices, such skills cannot be developed.

Let's think about the difference between the way a middle class family might go about purchasing a car and the way a family from poverty might go about purchasing a car. Yes, I mentioned in Chapter 9 that people in poverty have nice cars. Some do, but many do not.

In a poverty or low-income family there will be a certain amount of cash available to purchase a car. People in poverty usually do not qualify for loans. Usually the car that they are replacing has completely died and will not be able to be traded in or sold second hand. So, the family will have a certain amount of cash to buy a car. Usually, the car will be second hand. There will not be any discussions about what type of car would be suitable for the family or democratically voting on what color they would like the car to be. The parent or parents of the household would merely take the cash and go buy a car. Perhaps they wouldn't even buy a car; they would merely take a relatives "hand me down" car. Hence, there is no negotiating or decisions to be made among family members.

In a middle class family, there will be the option of paying cash or taking out a loan. There will also be the options of trading in the car that is already owned. The middle class family will visit the shops of a few different makes and styles of cars that suit their needs and interests. They might also look into second hand car options. They will consider if it is best to pay cash or take out a loan. If taking out a loan, they will consider how much the monthly installments will be vs. what their budget can afford. Maybe the husband thinks this type of car at this price is best for the family, while the wife feels that some other car suits the family's needs and budget. Meanwhile, the children in the family will also have ideas about what car would be best and in what color. Hence, there will be much, discussion and thinking.

Now, let's bring this one step further to a shelter home setting. In a shelter home, the teens are driven around in a large van, which is donated to the home by some charity or the government. It is a done deal, no choices, no discussion, no negotiating.

The best way to help hurt teenagers from poverty backgrounds is to help them build an adult voice as part of their language. This begins with giving them choices and teaching them the language of negotiation. The two main ingredients of effective communication and discipline with hurt teenagers is structure and choice. This moves the teen toward internal locus of control. The teen sees that he has a choice to behave or react in different ways and what the results of behaving or not behaving in a certain way will be. Some results will be positive and some will be negative. However, the choice remains with the teen.

When teens are communicated to or disciplined from the point-of-view of "I will tell you what to do, how to do it and when to do it," this doesn't leave any room for independent choice and thought.

Let's think about the following questions

What behaviors are needed for a teen to be successful?
Does the teen have those resources to develop these behaviors?
How will the behaviors be taught to the teen?
Does the teen have opportunities to make age appropriate choices?
What will help the child repeat successful behaviors?

Here are some common negative behaviors observed in hurt teenagers, followed by positive alternatives, which have to be modeled and taught to the hurt teen.

Laugh when disciplined – This is a coping mechanism. They don't want to show fear or concern. Understand where the laughter is coming from and ignore it. When other systems are in place the laughter will go away.

Argue loudly with authority figures – Remember, hurt teenagers don't trust authority figures. They view the adult as the enemy who is out to get them and does not believe in them. Simply tell the teen that all of this shouting isn't going to help solve anything. Can we please sit down and discuss this?

Angry response – This, too, is based on fear and a way to "save face" in the situation. When teens make inappropriate or vulgar comments, the teen is mimicking what he hears in his environment. Continue to model for him mature, positive responses to unpleasant situations.

Physical fights - This is necessary to survive in poverty. Hurt teens do not know how to use conflict resolution. Hurt teens see themselves as weak if they don't fight or fight back. Physical strength is an asset, especially when a teen is from an environment of poverty. It will take time and a lot of modeling before a hurt teen will understand that physical fighting is unacceptable and there are other acceptable means to settle disagreements.

Cannot follow directions – There is little procedural memory in poverty. Sequencing, planning ahead or organizing their time and energy is not used or valued. They are very much in the moment surviving.

Extremely disorganized – Plans are not made in poverty. Planning, scheduling and organizing are not skills taught in poverty. Many times, especially in poverty, hurt teens don't have a personal place to put things in the home.

Doesn't complete tasks – There is no procedural self-talk. They do not see the "whole task."

Help them understand procedural memory. Write the steps down and help them to organize the task in a step-by-step manner.

Harm others verbally or physically – Hurt teenagers tend to addresses issues in a negative way; again they are living out what they have experienced. Help them to know that there are other choices available, such as …

- Talk it out.
- What did you do?
- When you did that, what did you want?

- List four other things you could have done. This can be difficult for hurt teens because they honestly aren't able to see choices.
- What will you do next time.

Hurt teens will have the most difficulty with the third one. When they cheat or steal, this is about control or it could also be about what they feel they need and cannot get any other way. This happens as a result of weak role models and emotional resources. This also comes from little appropriate support and guidance in formative years. Help the teen understand that cheating is not acceptable and stealing is against the law.

When parents are still in the picture, generally speaking, hurt teens do not have healthy relationships with their parents. This is a large part of what makes them hurt. However, parents tend to get very possessive of their teenagers when some other significant adult enters the picture. It is important for mentors to "befriend" the parent. Hopefully, the parent will be grateful that the mentor is there. If not you are fighting a loosing battle.

Self- reflective Questions

1. What are some of the ways you have used to enter the world of teenagers?
2. Think back to the days when you were a teen. Who were the adults who knew how to enter your world? How did they enter your world?
3. Who were the adults whom you felt couldn't enter your world?
4. When speaking with teens, which of the three voices do you find yourself using, at what times, and under what circumstances?
5. Think of the teens you know and interact with on a frequent basis. What voices do you hear them using, at what times and under what circumstances?

Diana's Pearls of Wisdom – Teenagers will learn what they live; in turn, they will live what they learn. Hence, we as significant adults in their lives must model what it is we want them to live and learn.

CHAPTER FOURTEEN

Basic Counseling Skills 101

The Basic Counseling Process

As mentioned earlier, mentoring is a different relationship with your mentee than the relationship a counselor has with a client. However, as a mentor you will end up doing a lot of "counseling" with your mentee. Your mentee will begin discussing his feelings, fears, joys and concerns. Hence, it will be important to handle such conversations as would a counselor, as opposed to how a mother, father, friend, enemy, lover or teacher would respond.

If you are already a professional counselor, psychologist, social worker or psychiatrist, **GREAT,** please use your skills. All of the rest of you, no worries, here is a crash course; as for the seasoned mental health pros, indulge in a review.

The Significant Others Relationship Map

The first thing that I do with all clients and mentees (*regardless of age and situation*) is create a relational map of the significant people in the client or mentee's life and the interpersonal connection between the client or mentee and these people. This gives me a visual picture as to how the client or mentee's is "peopled." This is not done in front of the client or mentee. It might take a few sessions to get this information. Patience is important. There are many ways to do this map. This is my way.

Draw a Map

- Close relationships to the teen are represented by two thick lines.
- Medium relationships are represented by one thick line.
- Distressed relationships are a broken line.
- Abusive relationships are a zigzag broken line.
- Then you need to connect people to other people the same way.

The people and quality of interpersonal relationships can change over time; hence the map will need to be updated throughout your journey with your mentee.

Below are two examples of a Relationship Map

Again, there are many ways to do a graph. This is my way.

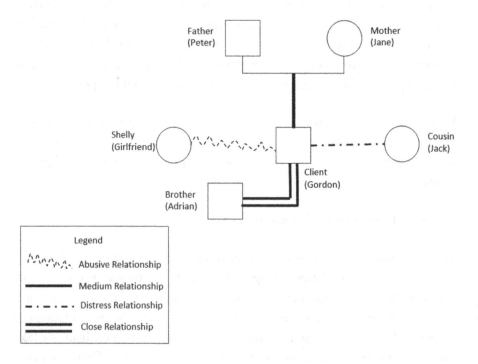

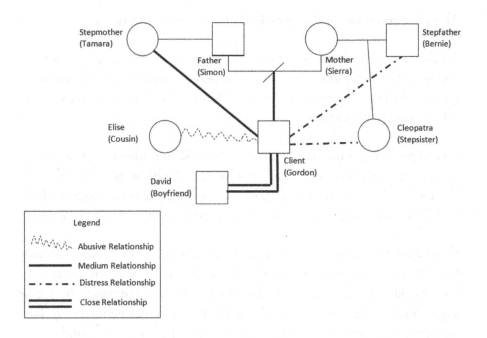

Open vs. Closed Questions

In counseling situations, we want to ask as many open questions as possible. Closed questions are also good and necessary at times; however, when counseling, the majority of questions should be open.

What is the difference between open and close questions?

Closed questions have either a yes or no answer or a specific answer. Such as, "Do you like to play golf?" The person will answer yes, no or it's OK. You probably won't get much conversation after that. For example, a question requiring a specific answer would be "When is your birthday?" I would answer this specific question by saying November 1st (*Feel free to send flowers, cards and gifts – SMILES*).

An open question requires an answer, which requires more thinking, reflecting and usually more information. Such as "Tell me about the different leisure activities you like?"

Also avoid **multiple-choice questions** and **either or questions**.

An **either or question** would be - "Does that make you happy or sad?" By asking either or questions, you limit the person's response. There are many types of feelings. Instead, ask the teen "How does that make you feel?" or "What feelings does that bring up for you?"

A **multiple - choice question** would be - "Would you rather go to the park, go swimming or stay home every day this summer?" Multiple choice questions are also limiting. Perhaps the teen doesn't want to do any of these. Instead ask the teen "If it were entirely up to you, what would you like to do this summer?"

Never lead the witness – What is leading the witness? This term is actually from the legal profession. During a court trial, lawyers will object when the lawyer from the other side leads the witness. We lead the person by asking a question in a way that makes him think in a way that he might not have thought on his own. This channels the person to have a certain mind set.

For example…

Teen: I hate to be in the house when my dad gets home from work. All he does is start screaming and yelling.

A Leading response: Does this make you angry? By saying angry, you have led the witness to think about being angry. There are many other feelings that teen might be experiencing.

Non-leading response: "What feelings does this bring up for you" or "How do you react when this happens?"

NOTE: your mentee (*and clients alike*) will get very **SICK** of the hearing the **FEELINGS** word. Please use to a minimum to avoid sounding like a broken record.

Another example would be…

Teen: I don't see why I need to be in school all day; all we do is sit in class and listen to the teacher go over the same thing, again – and again – and again.

Leading Statement: It sounds like you are bored in school. By saying bored, you have led the witness to think about being bored. There are many other feelings that teen might be experiencing.

Non-leading response: Any ideas about what would make school more interesting for you?

Sympathy vs. Empathy

Empathy is a key word in person-centered counseling. However, many people, even very experienced mental health professionals can't explain the difference between empathy and sympathy. They believe that they are being empathetic, when in reality, they are being sympathetic.

So, what is the difference?

First, let's review all four possible feelings.

Apathy is a total lack of caring. Sort of like when an ant is crawling toward your lunch plate and you smash it dead. This is apathy. You have no regard for the life of the ant, nor do you care. Your food is what is important and not the life of the ant.

Pity is feeling sorry for someone without being inclined to help in any way. Like when you see a picture of a mal-nourished child from a third world country and think, I am so blessed to be born in this country.

In the world of mental health, there is no place for apathy or pity.

Now we have **sympathy and empathy.**

Sympathy is to feel deeply for the person in his unfortunate situation and want to help in some way or be of solace. The feeling of sympathy lingers with you for a while. For example, when we sincerely respond to someone when he tells you that his father died by saying, "I am so sorry for your lose; you and your family are in my thoughts and prayers." Then we continue to think about the situation (*in the back of our minds, or maybe the front of our minds*) for several hours or the rest of the day.

Empathy is to feel the feeling that the person is experiencing and to be present with the person without trying to fix anything. Empathy also leaves the person feeling as though you have "shared" the experience with him. An example would be if you have ever seen a movie and the plot was about someone dying of cancer. At the beginning of the movie, we see a happy family with mom, dad, two kids and a dog. Then 30 minutes into the movie, the mom is diagnosed with stage four cancer. The rest of the movie is about the family living out the mother's last days of life. As the movie ends, all the family members are around Mom's deathbed crying and saying their last goodbyes. We then see the flat line on the heart monitor; Mom has passed. At this point, we are crying with the rest of the family members. We have become intertwined with the feelings and plight of the family.

Now you don't have to cry with your mentee to feel empathy; although, it is perfectly fine if you do. It is actually about the use of personal pronouns. When showing sympathy, we usually use 1st and second person pronouns, such as **you** and **I**. In the example above with sympathy, the person responded by saying "**I** am so sorry for **your** loss." The pronoun **"I"** is first person and **"your"** is second person. There is a separation between the two people involved when we use the pronouns, **I** and **you.** Now an empathetic response would be more like, "It is so devastating when **our** dear loved ones pass." The word **"our"** is a third person pronoun. By saying **"our"** we have joined in the feeling and/or situation with our mentee.

Let's look at the whole picture.

Imagine looking through a magazine and you see a picture of a starving and dirty child from a third world country. The caption reads, "Send your dollars to care."

An **apathetic** response would be to give it a quick glance and continue flipping the pages. The picture doesn't arouse any emotion within you.

A response of **pity** would be to look at the picture for a moment and think, "I am so blessed not to be born in that country under those situations." Then you flip the pages.

A **sympathetic** response would be to look at the picture, read what is involved in helping and think I wish that I could help, but my budget is too tight. Then the picture lingers in your mind for several minutes, hours or maybe even the rest of the day.

An **empathetic** response would be to look at the picture and say a prayer (*if you pray*) for the child and country. Then the picture lingers in your mind for several minutes, hours or maybe even the rest of the day.

Below are examples of sympathetic and empathetic responses; pay special attention to the use of personal pronouns.

Your best friend of ten years comes to you in tears and tells you that her fiancé has broken off the engagement because he just doesn't think he is ready to settle down.

A sympathetic response would be, "**I** am so sorry to hear this. **I** am here whenever **you** need to talk."

An empathetic response would be, "It is so hurtful when the person **we** planed to spend the rest of **our** lives with suddenly doesn't feel the same for **us**."

A high school teen, who is getting ready to graduate at the top of her class, comes to you in tears and says, "My parents are so disappointed in me because I didn't get a full scholarship to Harvard. I only received a partial scholarship. They said that I am the first to break the family legacy of going to Harvard on a full scholarship. They said that I should have participated in more extra-curricular activities."

A sympathetic response would be, "How can **your** parents not realize how hard **you** have worked. Any scholarship to Harvard is a great honor. **I** am surely proud of **you**."

An empathetic response would be, "It is very disappointing when **our** parents are so involved with their own hopes and dreams for **us** that they don't recognize and validate **our** hard work and efforts."

You are the mentor of a hurt teen who is trying to get back on track with his high school education. He calls you in tears because even after studying all week, he still didn't pass algebra and will have to repeat the course in summer school.

A sympathetic response would be, "So sorry to hear. Please remember that **you** did the best that **you** could and made excellent progress overall. **You** just need some more time with the course. **I** will be here to help **you** through summer school. Keep working hard and think positive. Math drove **me** crazy too.

An empathetic response would be, "Let **us** think positively. **We** scored 15 points higher than the last exam. **We** just need some more time and practice. **We** will keep up **our** study routine and get through the course this summer."

What did you notice as being the difference between the sympathetic personal pronouns and empathetic personal pronouns?

The **sympathetic pronouns** are either first person or second person – you, yours, me, I my. There is a separation between the two people.

The **empathetic pronouns** are third person inclusive - we, us, our. The two people are working as a team.

Simply put, sympathy allows the hurt person to know that we hear him, understand him and feel for him. Empathy allows the hurt person to know that you are experiencing the feelings and situation with him.

IMPORTANT: Empathy must be completely genuine and not just words. Sometimes, we can't be genuinely empathetic because we don't share the same love and commitment to what the hurt person is experiencing. So, how can we show empathy?

I am not a cat lover (*no offense anyone*). A very good friend of mine had a beautiful Persian cat named Fluffy for 11 years. She raised Fluffy ever since she was a six-week-old kitten. Whenever I would visit my friend, Fluffy would come and sit by my feet and rub up against my leg for a while. I would pet Fluffy and then she would roam off. I would then go to the bathroom and brush the long fur from my pants. Fluffy was beautiful, but because I am not a cat lover, I found Fluffy to be annoying most of the time. I loved Fluffy because of my love for my friend. My friend was aware of this.

When Fluffy died unexpectedly at the age of 11, my friend called me in deep bereavement. Now, I couldn't genuinely be empathetic and say, "I am so heartbroken that **our** beloved cat that **we** loved so much with **our** whole heart and soul is no longer with us." Although, I was very sad for my friend's loss.

So, I used what I call **Empathetic Validation.** I was sympathetic but also validated her feelings and love for Fluffy by saying, "I am so sorry to hear, **Fluffy was so blessed to have such an unconditionally loving caregiver her whole life**. My thoughts and prayers are with Fluffy." I then spent the next two days with my friend helping her build a memorial for Fluffy.

Try practicing empathy and empathetic validation in your day-to-day life – Good Luck.

Stop asking "Why" Questions – Why??

I remember working on my first master's degree in counseling back in the 80's. No worries, my friends, all the dinosaurs were dead and gone; we were learning how to counsel people. One of my favorite professors was teaching counseling techniques that semester. So, as is typical of such classes, we students were role-playing counseling sessions. Whenever the counselor asked the client a **"why"** question (*as well as other mistakes*) the professor would ring a bell. I quickly learned not to ask why questions. At that point, I also learned to not ask **"why"** questions in my day-to-day life. Whenever I hear someone asking a "why" question, it is like someone racking his fingernails down a blackboard; it sends chills down my spine. Blackboards…you know those old things teachers wrote on with dusty chalk until the mid 1990's. If not, you can Google them up on the web.

Back to **why** not ask **why** questions. Whenever we ask someone a why question, we are asking him to justify, defend or explain himself. I hate it when people ask me, "Why do you live in Malaysia." I feel like answering, "Why do you care?"

But sometimes we really want or need to know "why" about something. OK, fine, just change your language. Instead of asking "Why do you live in Malaysia?" Ask "What do you like about Malaysia?"

- Why did you choose that university?
- Why don't you like him?
- Why did you quit your job?
- Why are you always fighting with your brother?
- Why did you fail math this term?

Why – WHY – **WHY** – However, we might need the above information, so we merely change the wording.

For example:

- Why are you moving to a new house?
  Tell me more about your new house. What do you like best about your new house?
- Why did you choose that university?
  What attracted you to that university?
- Why did you quit your job?
  What happened with your job?
- Why are you always fighting with your brother?
  Any ideas what's causing all of your frustrations with your brother?
- Why did you fail math?
  What happened in math class this semester?

You will find that "non-why" questions open the door to more cooperative conversation. In the end, you will still learn why. The word "what" works well, but it is not the only word substitution.

Try to stop asking "why" questions in your day-to-day life –Good Luck.

Opinions and Advice

Never give opinions or advice, not even when asked. Merely facilitate your mentee's knowledge and understanding of his choices. Then help him explore what is best for him. Unless, of course, the teen is making a decision, which will put him in danger or he is considering breaking the law. If this is the case, by all means give advice.

If your mentee asks what you would do or choose in such a situation, answer by saying, "Which one I would do isn't important, what is important is for us to explore which is the best for you. So let's explore all of your options."

Personal Disclosure

This is always a very gray area. Simply put, only disclose when it is 100 % relevant to the teen's experience and the disclosure will help the teen. This usually comes with the territory of being a wounded healer.

IMPORTANT: Wounded healers are the **BEST** healers; however, the **wounded healer must be healed.** Can you imagine an alcoholic trying to help someone stay sober? The best mentors for hurt teens are "healed" hurt teens because a healed hurt teen has traveled the same journey as his mentee.

Back to personal disclosure - Again, if you do disclose, it should be solely for the benefit of your mentee. However, please remember that your mentee (*as would a client in the mental health profession*) doesn't carry the burden of confidentiality. So, whatever you tell the teen might be passed on to someone else. So always ask yourself, "Would I mind if he shared this with someone else?"

NEVER…. I repeat – Never… one more time - Never burden your mentee with a secret. For example, sharing something about yourself and then asking the mentee to keep it private. Now, of course, it is OK to disclose basic aspects of yourself that helps the teen get to know you as a person, such as if you have children, where you work, where you went to school, movies you like, etc.

Self-reflective Questions

1. When do you find yourself asking "why" questions? Practice asking without using the word "why."
2. What situations do you find yourself being sympathetic?
3. What situations do you find it difficult to be empathetic?
4. What are some techniques you use to enter a teen's world?
5. Practice being present for someone without trying to "fix" anything.

Diana's Pearls of Wisdom – Knowing that you have a genuine empathetic support system during your times of struggle is the biggest source of comfort.

CHAPTER FIFTEEN

Expressive Activities

Below are several expressive activities that teens like to do. Such activities help you to get to know your mentee better, but more importantly, they help your mentee to know himself better. Not all of the activities below will be suited for all teenagers. Please use much forethought and insight when choosing activities you believe to be the most suitable for your mentee.

Lifetime Journey

Begin with a large piece of art block and some stickers, colors, markers, etc. Have your mentee place a sticker some where on the page. This represents the time of his birth. He writes down everything he remembers (*actually has been told*) about his birth - the place, who was there, was it daytime or nighttime, etc.

Then ask him to place another sticker. This represents his third birthday. Between the birth sticker and the three years old sticker, your mentee writes down whatever he remembers (*or has been told*) about his life between the ages of birth and three. Were any new siblings born, did the family move, did he begin nursery school, etc.

Continue in three-year blocks, ages six, nine and twelve. When you get to age twelve, go year by year. These are very important years because at age twelve, we begin our early teen years, which is the time when social comparison and the development of a sense of self will begin.

Most people don't remember much about their first six years of life. You can ask your mentee to ask his parents, older siblings or relatives about what was going on in your mentee's life during those first six years. Also, looking at photographs or even videos can be a big help. Always remind the teen to share within his comfort zone.

Hurt children and teenagers usually have sad memories. This might be too difficult your mentee who have been traumatize. Use your better judgment. Maybe this activity would be OK at a later time.

Creative Journaling

Teens love this activity, especially the girls; however, boys enjoy creative journaling as well. Creative journaling is just what it says, being creative as you journal. This means to use different creative mediums to express your thoughts, feelings, fears, hopes, joys, concerns, etc. However, this is not the typical "Dear Diary" type journaling.

The first step is to have your mentee make the journal. To make the journal, take about 20 sheets or more of large blank, white art paper. Punch holes into the paper and tie together with some string or ribbon; have your mentor choose the color. Then have your mentee decorate the cover however he would like. This is all about self-expression.

Use the blank pages for collage making, drawings, mandalas, creative writing, etc. Here are some ideas.

1. The Me Collage: Have your mentee cut and paste pictures from magazines. He can also include original art drawings or doodling. He can use stickers, glitter or add on sequence, whatever he wishes. Afterwards invite the teen to share these different aspects of himself and how they are meaningful to him.

2. From Pictures to Stories: For this activity, you will need to have a large array of different pictures, such as abstract, concrete, people, places, things, childish pictures, adult pictures, etc. Where to get such pictures? They are everywhere - calendar pictures, postcards, magazines, greeting cards, newspapers, etc. Once you start looking for them and collecting them, you will find them everywhere. I always suggest laminating the pictures for long-term use.

You can either have your mentee take a picture from a grab bag, or show him about 10 to 20 pictures (*the more variety the better*) and ask the teen to choose the picture that interests him the most.

Your mentee then will make up a narrative of some sort about what he sees in the picture. This can be in any genre or form. Then he can put his words into writing. You can also ask facilitative questions to help the mentee along. Such as "When you look at this picture what do you see?" or "Imagine you are one of the people, places or things in this picture. Where do you see yourself." or "Imagine that you are going to place yourself in this picture. Where do you want to be?"

Then the next question is based on what he says. You can further facilitate by asking a question about his statement as need be. Such as what is the dog's name? What crossed Harry's mind when he saw the two-headed dragon? He can then bring the oral story to writing if he wishes to do so. You can also make this a collaborative project. Whereby the both of you are contributing to the story.

3. Story Starters: Give your mentee a beginning line and have him continue, such as…

- If I were King/Queen for a day…
- _____is the color of _____because….
- The best use for hand phones is….
- The rain makes me feel…
- If I could have any pet in the world, I would want a _____ because…
- My dream birthday celebration would be.

4. Mandala Coloring and Creating: As you probably know, mandalas are circular designs (*need not be a perfect circle*) with a center point. They are universal and can be found all around us. They can be seen on stain-glassed windows, plates, ceramic tiles, etc. They are present in many religious art works. Islamic art has many mandalas. The Tibetan monks spend years creating sand blown mandalas. Hindus call them "Yantras" and have them painted on the floor in front of their front doors as a welcoming symbol. Several people use them for meditation because they are so relaxing to look at. Sometimes they are symmetrical and sometimes they are not. Sometimes we doddle them and don't even know we are creating them.

You can also buy mandala coloring books and color them or you can create your very own original mandalas. You can even create them using pattern blocks. Don't limit the drawing tools to colors, markers and/or paints. Feel free to add in stickers, jewels, sequins, glitter, etc. The more craft materials to choose from, the better. When finished, your teen can give their mandala a title and express what it means to them.

Collaborative mandala making is also fun – see collaborative picture making a few activities down. It is the same concept.

5. **Free Drawing or Sketching:** This is always a good idea. Always invite your mentee (*however never insist*) to share what his drawing is about. He can also put his thought into writing.

6. **Add to a poem:** Find a poem that your mentee will be able to relate to in some way and have him add a sentence, a few lines or a stanza to the poem. Or, better yet, have your mentee suggest a poem that he likes.

For example: Let's look at the poem below by Robert Frost.

Nothing Gold Can Stay
by Robert Frost

Nature's first green is gold,
Her hardest hue to hold.
Her early leaf's a flower;
But only so an hour.
Then leaf subsides to leaf,
So Eden sank to grief,
So dawn goes down to day
Nothing gold can stay.

Added stanza by Diana
So, I will appreciate what is here today
And enjoy it in every way
Nothing gold can stay.

If your mentee had made up this stanza, he could then reflect on what is "gold" in his life and discuss why he believes it won't stay. Also, your mentee can make up his own original poems and reflect upon them. Illustrations are always welcome.

7. **Song Lyrics:** Have your mentee write down the lyrics to his favorite songs and then illustrate them. Have your mentee and/or write a reflection of what the song's message is for him. If applicable, have your mentee write in the name of the person into the song lyrics that he is mad at, in love with, wants to apologize to, etc. or something he wants to stop doing or avoid in his life.

For example: below are a few lines from a song by Craig David.

I'm Walking Away **(Wild star Recordings – 2000)**

"I'm walking away, from troubles in my life. I'm walking away, oh, to find a better day."

Change to:

"I'm walking away from **marijuana** in my life, I walking away, oh, to find a better day, etc."

8. **Happy Heart – Broken Heart:** This activity can be done with both hearts in the same session or only one, whatever is most appropriate to your mentee and what he is working through.

Happy Heart: Draw an outline of a big heart. Have your mentee write or draw what makes him happy inside of the heart, including people, places and things. Discuss how your mentee can have more of these people, places and things in his life that make him happy. Is there something that he is doing to stop himself from having these people, places and things in his life that make him happy? What is in his control and what is not in his control?

Broken Heart: Draw an outline of a broken heart. Have your mentee write or draw what makes him unhappy inside of the broken heart, including people, places and things. Discuss how your mentee can avoid these people, places and things in his life that make him broken hearted. Is there something that he is doing that keeps these heartbreaking people, places and things in life that make him unhappy? What is in his control and what is not in his control?

Clay Modeling

Paper clay is very earthy and moldable. There is a therapeutic quality about being able to roll, squeeze, punch, smash, or pound the clay. Your mentee can mold it into whatever he would like. This is often done without any forethought. Your mentee begins to mold and then something eventually emerges. Your mentee can paint the creation after it dries for a few days.

Sometimes I direct this activity by saying to make any type of container. Then I discuss what the teen would like to contain in his container. This can be an affirmation, a goal, dream, small keep sakes, etc.

Collaborative Pictures

I have found that even teenagers who aren't keen on drawing or art work like this activity. Begin with some large, plain white art paper and an array of colors, color pencils and markers. You begin by drawing a random line, curve or swiggle on the page and then ask your mentee to add something to it. Then you add some thing to that and then he adds something and the two of you go back and forth until the creation is finished. No need to discuss it or make comments about it along the way.

The two of you will know when the picture is finished. When you are finished, you can ask your mentee what the picture reminds him of. Usually this will open up the door to discussion about something significant to the teen. If your mentee says that he doesn't know and asks you what the picture reminds you of, go ahead and say something. However, keep it superficial. This usually motivates your mentee to explore his or her thoughts about the picture. The idea is for your mentee not to be influenced by what you see in the picture, remember not to "lead the witness."

Vision Boards

This is easy and fun for teens. Give your mentee a large piece of art paper or poster paper (*the bigger the better*) and have your mentee draw or cut and paste from magazines (*or both*) pictures that depict where he would like to be in five years. Some hurt teens might not be able to think that far ahead, so you can say when you finish high school. Then process what your mentee creates.

Hypothetical Independent Living

This happens in several steps. Also, this activity should be done when a solid rapport has been built with your mentee. This is done from the point-of-view that your mentee has graduated from high school and is living on his own.

Step One: Have your mentee find a job for which he is qualified. Look in the newspaper or on the windows of stores at the mall. It will be something like Mc Donald's or a department store. Calculate how much money he can make working a 20 – 40 hour week (*does he want to work full or part-time*). If he wants more education, he will only be able to work part time. So now he has a monthly income.

Step Two: Your mentee has to find a room to rent; he can find in the paper. Have your mentee deduct his rent from his salary. I always recommend that your mentee find a room close to work to save on transportation fees.

Step Three: Have your mentee make up a grocery list of what he likes to eat; this also has to include toiletries, trash bags, cleaning supplies, etc. Then go hypothetically shopping; meaning, go to the store and see the prices but don't buy anything. No worries, he will quickly learn that he can't afford Mc Donald's every day. Then deduct these expenses from his salary. Usually your mentee is in the hole by this time, even the ones who work full-time. So he has to make adjustments in terms of the brands he uses, the food he eats; sacrifice – sacrifice – sacrifice - that's the reality of the adult world. We don't always get what we want, when we want it and how we want it.

Step Four: If your mentee is looking to pursue higher education or job training skills, help your mentee find out about scholarships, sponsorships, low-cost loans, etc. This, too, becomes part of his hypothetical living activity. This activity never fails to be a real eye opener. Especially if you are working with shelter home teens who are accustomed to the food track coming and delivering food, free of charge every week. They are very shocked at the thought of buying their own food and paying their own way through life.

Life Size Portraits

Teens really enjoy creating the life size portrait. This activity works well because it gives your mentee an opportunity to share his self-perception. Sometimes the teen does this at a conscious level, other times it is unconscious and of course, a combination of both. Take a very large roll of banner paper, or butcher paper and cut off a piece several centimeters longer than your mentee.

Have your mentee lie down on the paper in any position be would like. Trace the outline of your mentee's body. Your mentee then decorates the picture however he would like. Some teens will decorate themselves very realistically, others will decorate themselves worse than they are, such as fatter.

Many teens will decorate their fantasy self, meaning, how they wish they were. Sometimes it is what the teen hopes to become or is working on becoming. Sometimes the teen realizes this is a fantasy, other times he doesn't. Whatever the outcome is, it doesn't matter. Based on clinical observation, the stronger the teen's sense of self, the more realistic he will represent himself. The weaker the sense of self, the more unrealistic the teen will represent himself.

When your mentee finishes, you can ask him to share his thoughts. Just enter his world and go with his thoughts and feelings. Invite your mentee to write his thoughts in his creative journal and put a picture of his portrait in his journal. I have also found it beneficial to do to this activity again six months to a year later in order to see if the teen represents himself differently. Usually, the teen does, and it is interesting to see how his self-perceptions have changed. Remember, most teens love it when the mentor joins in the activity. So, I recommend doing the same activity with yourself alongside your mentee.

Movie Characters or Characters from Novels

A great way to understand the inner desires, fantasies, dreams, hopes or anger is to connect with the fictional characters (*whether real people or cartoon characters*) that he identifies with from either books or television. In this day and age, it is usually television, but this is OK. We identify with such characters because we see ourselves in the character, or we want to be like the character, meaning the character is empowered in some way that we wish we were empowered.

Once your mentee identifies the character, invite your mentee to put the character in some sort of concrete form, by drawing a picture of the character, finding the character on the net and printing a hard copy, or finding a three-dimensional figure of the character.

Then invite the teen to share about the following:

- What about this character resonates with you?
- What do you admire about this character?
- Is there anything about this character that you would like to change?
- What quality does your mentee believe that he shares with the character?
- If you could change something about this character, what would it be? because.....
- Imagine that you are going to be a new character in the movie, how do you see yourself playing a part in this movie?

Processing your Mentee's Expressive Work

Inner Witnessing vs. Outer Witnessing

There are two levels of processing expressive work. There is inner witnessing and there is outer witnessing. What is the difference between the two?

Inner Witnessing

Inner witnessing takes place when the creator of the work processes his work through self- reflecting. Each person can only be his own inner witness. No one can inner witness for anyone else. Each individual person is his own inner witness. Through self-reflection, the creator expresses the thoughts and feelings portrayed in his work, as well as the overall meaning of his work, as he is experiencing it in the here and now. This processing can also be facilitated by way of the mentor asking facilitative, open questions about the work.

It is important to remember the following…

- Do not call the work or any part of the work anything until the creator identifies it. For example, you might look at your mentee's creation and see a house. Please do not call it a house until the creator of the work calls it a house. Maybe to the creator, it is not a house – it is something else.
- Do not identify a color until the creator does. People see colors in different ways.

If you do either of the above, you would be "leading the witness. Remember – very important – **NEVER LEAD THE WITNESS.**

The inner witness always goes first. Never allow outer witnessing until the creator has inner witnessed his creation.

Outer Witnessing

Outer witnessing takes place when someone other than the creator of the work processes the work from his own point of view. Always begin outer witnessing by saying …

As I put myself in your creation, I feel, I think…
As I put myself in your story, I feel, I think…
As I put myself in your situation, I feel, I think….

When we serve as an outer witness, we share how the situation makes us feel in an empathetic way. Please be careful, the purpose of being an outer witness is not to say what you believe the mentee to be feeling and experiencing, but to share your thoughts and feelings as if you were truly in that situation. The feelings might be similar or the same (*in whole or in part*) as your mentee, or they may be totally different. Your mentee will let you know.

What is the purpose of serving as an outer witness? It allows the mentee to experience your connection with his situation. It shows him that you can relate to his experience and that you too have feelings and thoughts about the situation. **PLEASE BE CAREFUL**, if you know that the way your mentee's work makes you feel will upset him for some reason, don't share.

Don't outer witness in a way that is judgmental or negative. Such as...

"As I put myself in this story, I feel like I want to go and kill the person."

Instead say,

"As I put myself in this story, I feel intense anger building up inside of me."

Again, do not merely say what you think your mentee is feeling, thinking or experiencing. The purpose of outer witnessing is to express your "human" feelings. As a result, the mentee is given a chance to self-reflect and explore to what extent he has similar or different feelings.

Example: Your mentee shares the following. This example is from the viewpoint of verbal counseling and not processing expressive work.

I am so upset with my friend, Sue. Every time we make plans together, she changes the plans in some way at the last minute. We had plans to go see a movie together last Saturday. I had an opportunity to do some work with my uncle and make some extra money, but I really wanted to spend time with Sue. So, I put Sue first and told my uncle that I wasn't available. I was really looking forward to seeing the movie and spending time with Sue. I chose the outfit that I wanted to wear, and I had my sister French braid my hair that morning. I was so excited. Then one hour before we were supposed to meet at the mall, she sent me a text message and said she wanted to change to another day because she decided to go with her family to her cousin's house.

OK, so maybe it was important for her to go to her cousin's house, but then there have been other times when we make plans and she is late or she brings another friend along when it was supposed to be just the two of us. Sometimes she forgets her money and says she will pay me back, then she doesn't.

Mentor: As I put myself in your story, I feel like I am the one who is putting out all the effort and Sue isn't respecting my feelings in this relationship.

Then your mentee will respond in some way. You can then explore the following:

- What are the things that you enjoy about your friendship with Sue?
- How did the friendship develop?
- How do your other friends tend to treat you in these situations?
- How might you express your feelings to Sue.

It sounds like your mentee has a difficult time expressing her feelings. This can be typical of people with low self- esteem because they are probably used to being mistreated. Further work in exploring ways for your mentee to have a better self-care system is important.

REMEMBER: There is never any outer witnessing until the creator of the work first serves as his own inner witness. The creator has the right to say that he doesn't want outer witnessing. Let this be fine. The creator also has the right not to inner witness his work. Sometimes, people (*of all ages*) create an expressive work and then decide that they do not wish to share anything about it at that time. This is fine. Everything happens within the comfort zone of your mentee – **ALWAYS AND FOREVER.**

Board Games Teenagers Like to Play

Playing games with teenagers is a fun way to break the ice. Many hurt teens have never had an adult take the time to play a game with them. Playing games will also give you further insights into your mentee, such as how he handles winning or loosing, how does he strategize, is he OK with having to wait his turn or not always being first. Does he allow himself to just have fun with the game without worrying about winning or loosing?

Some suggested games include....

- Jenga
- Connect Four

- Congkat (*Mancala – its called in the west*)
- Checkers
- Chess
- Blockus
- Uno
- Traditional Card Games - Fish, Rummy, Battle, Black Jack

Self-reflective activities:

Try some (*or better yet, try ALL*) of the above activities and see where the journey takes you.

Diana's Pearls of Wisdom – Remember that your needs are just as important as the person's for whom you are mentoring. Don't forget to take care of yourself. **INDULGE** yourself with massages, yoga class, tap dance, shoot basketball loops, go shopping (*beware of situational poverty*) whatever allows you to rejuvenate yourself – **ENJOY.**

PARTING WORDS

Thanks for taking time to read my book. I hope that you have found the information enlightening and are even more motivated to join the ranks of helping hurt teenagers...front line infantry is always the best spot. Please let us all remember that the teenage years is all about cultivating a sense of self...ideally, a true sense of self.

To cultivate a true sense of self, one must have high self-esteem. For high self-esteem is the essential ingredient, which propels us to try, try again, take risks in the face of adversity, reach a bit higher than our grasp, admit our mistakes, own our behavior, realize our strengths and limitations, genuinely put aside our own needs and care for others in need and immediately set a new and higher goal in motion once one has been accomplished. For, this is the journey of self- actualization, which enables us to contribute positively to society at large.

Wishing everyone the best as we go forth and help Teens !!!!
Diana, October, 2016

DISCUSSION OF THE DISCUSSION QUESTIONS

Chapter One – Who are the hurt teens?

Discussions to the activity beginning on page 2

Teen A

Teen A is hurt and is in the beginning stage of trouble if he isn't quickly redirected. Teen A comes from an affluent home. His parents are professionals, and he has material comforts and an extended family member who cares. However, he is now on a slippery slope. Mom and Dad are busy with their high-powered careers and forgetting that even though Teen A is now a teenager, he still needs their emotional attention and involvement in his life. Currently he is only skipping tutoring sessions; however, this can easily progress to other, more dangerous rebellious behaviors. Also, hanging around video arcades can often times lead to trouble as well.

Needed resource - It would be best if Teen A's parents would rethink their busy career life and realize that teenagers also need parental support, guidance and emotional connection.

Teen B

Teen B is not hurt. Although Teen B is from a low socio-economic household, she is very productive, has emotionally available caregivers, and she is making future plans about post secondary education. Furthermore, she is not afraid to work in order to earn money for the church trip.

Resources – Teen B not only has strong familial support from her mother and grandmother, but she also has the support of positive adults from her church. I assume the adult leaders at the church are a positive influence because they are organizing trips for the youth group. Please beware, some church leaders abuse children and teenagers, both directly and indirectly. Have your microscopes ready.

Teen C

Teen C is hurt and far from being "out of the woods." He is making some good choices and is on a good path at this point. However, it is very typical for troubled teens fresh out of juvenile detention centers to be highly motivated. The memory of Juvie is still very fresh on their minds. Unfortunately, this fades with time. Also, the other big red flag is that Teen C is still associating with his old friends. To make a permanent change, troubled teens have to be willing to "change their playmates and their playground." Teen C is on the right path, but he will need continuous guidance and help to stay on the right path.

Resources Needed: A consistent adult mentee who understands street kids. Also a mentee who can help Teen C find a new playground and new playmates.

Teen D

Teen D is not hurt. All is going well in her life.

Resources: Teen D has a strong family bond. Her parents place an emphasis on family togetherness.

Teen E

Teen E is hurt. She comes from a prominent, well-to-do family, which requires her to have a certain social image and maintain a legacy. Teen E is playing the game pretty well so far, but the rebelliousness of her situation is beginning to creep in. She is talking to the boy of the enemy family. Hopefully, this isn't the beginning of a modern day Romeo and Juliet story (*I mean tragedy*).

Resources Needed: It would be ideal if Teen E's parents would become enlightened and understand the importance of Teens E evolving into her unique self. Currently, her parents are grooming her to carry out the family's aristocratic legacy. Remember the movie, *The Stepford Wives*? Well here we have a Stepford Kid…. scary.

Teen F

Teen F is not hurt. Dad has done a wonderful job being a single dad. Hopefully, Dad will agree to Teen F taking a couple of years to join Habitat for Humanity. If not, this could be the beginning of a strained relationship between the two, which could lead to rebellious behaviors.

Resources: Teen F has a great Dad who has his priorities straight. Hopefully, Dad won't jeopardize this strong bond by not being supportive of Teen F's desire to join habitat for humanity.

Teen G

Teen G is hurt and like Teen A, she is in the beginning stages of trouble if intervention is not implemented. The family moved at a very difficult stage in Teen G's life. It is hard for teenagers to move and change schools. Unfortunately, the parents didn't consider this.

Resources Needed: Teen G's parents need to understand adolescent development and make family decisions accordingly. It wasn't wrong for Teen G's Dad to take a new job, which pays more money; however, the children needed to be better emotionally prepared for the change.

Teen H

Teen H is hurt. He is living in a dysfunctional family and his way of dealing with it is to submerge and ignore the chaos around him. Although this keeps him out of trouble, he is harboring a lot of implosive anger that will one day erupt. I wonder if the only reason he wants to join the Marines is to play with guns? Has he explored his own talents, interests and proclivities?

Resources Needed: Teen H needs a consistent mentor who can help him explore his proclivities and begin to develop a true sense of self.

Teen I

Teen I is hurt. Her mother doesn't seem to be able to keep her safe or make "good choices" where the men in her life are concerned. Teen I is putting herself at risk for the sake of her mother's happiness. However, this happiness will be short lived; Mom will soon find out what the boyfriend is doing.

Resources Needed: Like Teen H, Teen I needs a consistent mentor who can help Teen I explore and discover her true sense of self. Presently, Teen 1 is giving up her own needs for the sake of Mom's happiness. However, with this guy, Mom will not be happy in the end. Teen H is the perfect example of a child or teen (*like most children and teenagers*) who will abandon himself for the sake of a parent. The underlying feeling is if Mom is happy, she will love me.

Which Teens are the most hurt?

Teen C and Teen I - When taking into consideration a true sense of self and Ruby Payne's personal resources, these two teens are the most at risk. Teen C is beginning to make better choices and acquire personal resources, but he will continue to need a lot of encouragement and guidance to continue on a positive path. Teen I needs a mentor who can help her to think of herself and her own life as she grows into a young adult.

Which Teens are at the least risk for becoming hurt?

Teens B and Teen D – When taking into consideration a true sense of self and Ruby Payne's personal resources, these two teens are the least at risk. They both have had consistent positive support systems their whole lives. Furthermore, the support system is within the immediate family system, which is the best place to find one's support system.

Chapter Two - Sense of Self

Discussions to the activity beginning on page 7.

Teen 1

This teenager seems to have a very realistic sense of self. He knows his talents, interests and proclivities, and he has realistic plans for his future.

Teen 2

This Teenager does not seem to have a sense of self. He seems out of touch with himself, with the exception of enjoying soccer. Unfortunately, he isn't being given the opportunity to explore and discover. Hence, he falls back on the only thing that is a somewhat familiar, working at a gas station.

Teen 3

This teenager has a basic understanding of her interest and has some aspirations. It is important that she begins to talk to people who are working in the bridal field and seeing what type of education is needed and what is involved when working in this line of business.

Teen 4

This teenager doesn't seem to have a strong sense of self. She is merely doing what she has been told her whole life that she should do. It is interesting that she is studying medicine but didn't say anything about enjoying science class. Is she merely reacting to her early programming that she should be a doctor. She does have some sense of self in that she realizes that she enjoys debating. It would be an interesting experience for her if she explored studying law; she likes debating.

Chapter 3 – Attachment

Discussions to the activity beginning on page 27.

Teenager X and Z are securely attached and Teenager Y is not. The families of Teenagers A and C are interested in one another's lives and what each is doing. They take time to listen to each other and don't mind setting aside their own interests in order to hear what someone else is doing. Teenager Y is not securely attached. His father is not setting aside his television to listen to his son. He is more concerned about his son's grades.

Chapter 6 – James Marcia

Discussions to the activity beginning on page 52.

Ricky – Moratorium – Ricky is a very active teen with a strong sense of self. He has many interests, he just isn't sure at this point what he wants to focus on. During his gap year, he would benefit from career exploration and perhaps career guidance counseling. Part of career guidance counseling should focus on his feelings about his volunteer work during his gap year. The activities that he has chosen to do during his gap year will serve to give him much information about what he most enjoys.

Alice – Foreclosure – Alice has ambitions; however, she suppresses them in order to honor what she believes to ne family loyalties. If Alice does not begin to explore her desires for a different lifestyle, she will likely live a life of regret.

Tara – Identity Achievement – Tara knows her life's passion. Although it doesn't seem that she has explored much else, when children have a natural gift they need not explore further. Where ever her travels take her, she will likely have ice-skating as a predominant part of her life. Perhaps one day, she will open her own ice-skating school.

Roger – Moratorium – Roger, being a child of the streets, finally has a support system through his church. If he remains with this support system, he can begin to discover his true self.

Lily- Identity Achievement – Lily has made a decision based on her interests, and she has explored the opportunities to pursue her interest in going to nursing school.

Billy – Moratorium - Billy is in touch with his interests; however, he is still deciding which to pursue.

Sabrina – Identity Diffusion/Potential for Moratorium

Identity Diffusion- Sabrina is not in touch with her interests because she hasn't had time to be a teenager. She has lived her life surviving from day-to-day in a very dysfunctional household.

Potential for Moratorium – Sabrina does mention that she will eventually look for a job. At this point she really doesn't know where to begin. She will need help to even begin to know where to explore and discover.

Rob – Identity Achievement – Rob is in touch with his interests and is well on his way to building a career for himself, a true entrepreneur.

Sally – Identity Diffusion – Sally has no desire to explore her interests; she is only interested in living her life day-to-day as a wealthy person.

Stephen – Moratorium/Foreclosure – Stephen is still exploring his true place within his church life and possible ministry. The fact that Stephen has been isolated within his community could be viewed as foreclosure.

Lucy – Moratorium – Lucy is in touch with her interests; she is trying to decide which one to pursue.

Daniel - Foreclosure/Identity Achievement - This one is debatable. It would seem like foreclosure because Daniel hasn't been exposed to any thing other than his Father's law office. However, like Tara's ice-skating, maybe this is his true life's calling, and he doesn't need anything more.

Chapter 8 – Parenting and Leadership Styles

Discussions to the activity beginning on page 76.

For all of the case scenarios we can assume that...

The Dictating Parent – will not seek to understand what caused the teenager to act dishonestly, irresponsibly or wanting to make a poor choice, which isn't age appropriate. The parent will merely respond to the teenager in a punitive or chastising manner.

The Dictating Ghost Parent – will do the same but from long distance communication, via e-mail, phone call or Skype call.

The Doormat Parent – will eventually give in and not help the teenager to make age-appropriate choices or own his own behavior. Hence, the teenager does not grow or learn from his decisions or actions.

The Ghost Parent – doesn't know what is going on, doesn't care, etc. So now, let's look at how the Bonded Parent would handle the situations.

1. I found this test in your drawer when I was putting your clothes away. I don't remember you showing me this test; can we talk about it?
2. As you know, I take your pack back to the dry cleaners every other month. I found this when I was emptying your backpack to bring it to the cleaners. Can we talk about it. Then after discussion say that the next time, you will have to report to the police because possession of it is against the law. *This will not apply if cannabis is legal in your state or country.*
3. If the bonded parents have a set age for dating, such as 16 and older, then no the girl shouldn't be allowed to go one-on-one with the boy as a date. If this isn't the case, the bonded parent would find out the details about the school dance, including how it will be chaperoned. Then meet the boy and his parents.
4. "I smell smoke around you; what is this about?" If the teen makes up some story that can't be true, say, "I don't believe that." Make it clear that smelling like smoke is not allowed in the house, and you hope that he will make the intelligent decision not to smoke considering all the facts about health risks. This will be more difficult if the parents are smokers. It's always hard to preach and be heard when we are not practicing the same.
5. First explore what is making the teenager want to drop out of school. Then discuss that dropping out of high school isn't allowed, but the

teenager is welcome to apprentice and/or volunteer at a auto mechanic shop on weekends for a few hours.

6. Listen to the teenager's reasons and say this is fine, but she will have to find a job and/or productive volunteer work in order to have an informal learning experience while continuing to explore what he would like to do. After one year, if she is still not ready to go commit to a course of study, she should be charged rent to live at home or have responsibilities to earn his keep.

7. Get all the information on the business venture and then make an intelligent business decision. If it is a sound business and good investment, have the teenager research options to pay for college, such as possible scholarships or low interest loans.

8. Explain that tattoos are permanent and that until she is self-supporting, only temporary tattoos are allowed.

9. Explain that the cuts concern you and discuss seeing a qualified mental health professional. Even if the cuts are not serious, it is a cry for attention. Hence the question is "Why does the teenager seek attention?" In the end, seeing a mental health professional is not an option. It is important that the parents also be involved in the therapy process.

10. Immediately call the police and put out a search for him. When he is found and brought home, have a very long talk about what this was all about. Then because he has lost your trust, investigate where he says he is going, with whom and for what reason until mutual trust is reestablished. Also whatever friends he was involved with, he should no longer be allowed to associate with them.

11. Ask the teenager what the symbol means and where he saw it or learned about it. Also spend time educating the child about gangs and gang involvement.

12. Honor the teenagers wishes to follow his passion.

What would a bonded mentor do? Activity from page 77.

1. Although a mentor wouldn't be looking in the teenager's drawers, if he found a hidden test with a failed grade, he would discuss it with the teen and help the teen share the grade with his caregivers. The bonded

mentor would also help the teen find the resources to get appropriate help in the subject matter.

2. Discuss the dangers and legality of smoking marijuana or having procession of it. Help the teenager find the appropriate mental health professional if he is using or abusing. Remind him that marijuana is against the law you have the responsibility to report it if found again, assuming that it is against the law in your state or country.

3. Discuss with the teenager the personality of the boy and how she knows the boy. Ask what her caregiver's rules are about dating. If it is OK for the girl to go with the boy as a date, discuss with her how to keep herself safe on the date.

4. Say that you smell smoke around him and ask how this is so. If he admits to smoking, discuss with him the health risks of smoking.

5. Discuss with the teenager what makes him want to drop out of high school. Take the teen to different automobile mechanic training programs and see what the requirements are. Also help him set up some volunteer hours at an automobile shop.

6. Help the teen find a job and the needed resources to sustain himself.

7. This probably wouldn't be a situation of a teen in the mentor program. But if so, talk the situation over with the teen and his parents, as above.

8. Discuss that tattoos are permanent.

9. Say the cuts concern you and help the teen find an appropriate mental health professional.

10. Immediately report to the police and caregivers.

11. Ask the teenager what the symbol means. If he is aware that it is a gang symbol, discuss the dangers of being involved in gangs and/or portraying the symbols of a gang.

12. Although this wouldn't be a situation that a mentee would encounter, honor his wishes.

Discussions for mentee situations from page 77.

1. It is best to confront the situation and invite discussion. Help the teen to find the appropriate professional help. Bring the caregiver into the discussion in order help with the situation. Remember that it is part of informed consent that if the teen is breaking the law (*in this case under-aged drinking*) you have a duty to report.

2. It is best not to comment or respond in any way to the dress. Explain to her what you feel is a comfortable sitting distance. Say that you feel more comfortable with handshakes or high fives. Even if you are comfortable with hugs, this girl feels sexual; hence, hugging is inappropriate.

3. The first step should be to discuss the matter with the caregiver and together report to the appropriate school authorities. Also investigate if the girl had anything to do (*directly or indirectly*) with the boy "choosing" her to be the girl he sends the notes too. Was she leading the boy on in anyway?

4. It is important to become educated about gender dysphoria and help him to find the appropriate mental health professional. Hopefully his parents or caregivers will become educated as well and be supportive in an appropriate manner.

5. First, try to find out who the friend is and for what reason the friend is giving her these earrings. If indeed the girl has been shoplifting, with the support of the caregiver, have the girl return the earrings to the store manager and apologize. She must pay for the earrings through community service. It is the stores decision whether or not they will press charges.

6. Regardless of what genders are involved, explain to the teen that the relationship will always be that of a mentor/mentee.

7. First investigate the personality of the boy and get the factual data.

8. Help your mentee find the appropriate mental health professional.

9. Tell your mentee what you have heard and have him tell you. Help him find academic help.

Chapter Nine – Poverty

Discussions to the activity beginning on page 88.

Kumar and Licha

Resources
Financial – Financial resources are very low and unstable
Education – general education
Physical – drinking problem

Emotional – doesn't have a support system
Role Model – none
Spiritual – none

Kumar is a parentified teen; he has to take care of a disabled younger sister. Mother is trying her best, but is stressed and has a drinking problem. Kumar needs to be allowed to be a teen.

Mom also needs a mentor; she can get support to go back to school and learn a skill to make more money; she should also take Kumar's father to court for child support. Getting help for her drinking problem, which is how she self-medicates, would also be helpful.

Ling Ling and Su Lin

Resources
Financial - Low; however getting better due to the settlement from the accident
Educational – OK
Physical - OK
Emotional – Support of church group friends
Role Models - perhaps some at church
Spiritual – church

Ling Ling - There is the issue of peer isolation, Ling Ling is not socializing or being encouraged to socialize with her peers. There is the secret about her mother. Ling Ling is now at an age where she can understand her mother's situation. She has the right to know the truth and decide whether or not she wants to try to contact her mother. This should all be done under the guidance of a qualified mental health professional. Grandmother is doing better but needs to be firm with church members. It is typical of people in poverty to feel that if one person comes into money, he should help others. It is important for Su Lin to keep the best interests of herself and Ling Ling in the forefront and not lend the money. As the saying goes, "Charity begins at home."

Afiq and Norani
Financial - Low
Educational - Low

Physical – Very Low
Emotional – Low
Role Models – Low
Spiritual – High – However, at this point, Afiq is not really connecting with the faith.

Afiq is a parentified child. Afiq needs time to be a teenager. The family needs help. Father needs to pay support and take responsibility for the needs of his family; however, it isn't likely that he will "see this." Sorry to say but Dad is a GI[2]. He is covertly abusing his family. Mother needs help to realize this. If we are lucky, Dad will be more empathic now that Mom is gravely ill. Does Dad have the capacity to be empathetic???

Liz and Cindy
Financial – Low
Educational – OK
Physical – Good
Emotional - Low
Role Models – None
Spiritual – None

Cindy is a very hurt teen who needs professional help, **IMMEDIATELY.** Cindy's mother continues to traumatize her by making boyfriend's a priority over child. Monitoring of Cindy's boyfriend is also recommended.

INDEX

C

O

P